THE SERMON
ON THE MOUNT

SUNY Series in Religious Studies
Robert C. Neville, Editor

Carl G. Vaught

THE SERMON ON THE MOUNT

A Theological Interpretation

State University
of New York Press

Quotations from the Bible are from the *Master Study Bible: New American Standard* (copyrighted 1982, by the Holman Bible Publishers, Nashville, Tennessee, 37234).

Published by
State University of New York Press, Albany

For information, address State University of New York
Press, State University Plaza, Albany, N.Y., 12246

Library of Congress Cataloging in Publication Data

Vaught, Carl G., 1939–
    The Sermon on the mount.

    (SUNY series in religious studies)
    Bibliography: p.
    Includes index.
    1. Sermon on the mount—Theology.   I. Title.
II. Series.
BT380.2.V38   1986   226'.906   86-14500
ISBN 0-88706-364-0
ISBN 0-88706-365-9 (pbk.)

10 9 8 7 6 5 4 3 2 1

FOR MY FATHER AND MOTHER

Contents

PART III

SIX EXPRESSIONS OF PERFECTION

PART IV

FINAL CONSIDERATIONS ABOUT GOD'S KINGDOM

PREFACE

With the possible exception of John 3.16, no Biblical text is more widely known or widely quoted than the Sermon on the Mount. Who has not heard the words, "Blessed are the meek, for they shall inherit the earth," "Blessed are the pure in heart, for they shall see God," or "Blessed are the peacemakers, for they shall be called the children of God"? And who has not repeated the phrase, "You are the salt of the earth," or bridled under the admonition to turn the other cheek and to love your enemies? Indeed, a strong defense could be made for the thesis that phrases like these reflect the essence of the Christian faith and that the Sermon on the Mount is the locus classicus of the teachings of Jesus. The Lord's prayer is to be found there; the distinction between treasures on earth and treasures in heaven and the claim that we cannot serve both God and mammon is formulated in this context; and the prohibition against anxiety and against the self-righteous condemnation of others is expressed within this framework. As the Sermon moves toward its conclusion, we are also confronted by a narrow gate and a narrow pathway which Jesus says that few can either enter or travel, and we are faced with two alternative ways of living, one of which founds human life upon a rock, while the other is content to build upon the sand. It is this familiar choice which the Sermon as a whole poses for its listeners, and it is the need to make a choice of this kind that has caused the multitudes who have listened to the message of Jesus "to be amazed at his teaching."

Despite the fact that the Sermon on the Mount is such a familiar document, the text has often been radically misconstrued. It has sometimes been understood as a humanistic manifesto that is universally accessible, pointing to what is best about the natural human consciousness. According to an interpretation of this kind, the Sermon is addressed to mankind as a whole, projecting the possibility that human beings can express their essential nature by living in the light of its requirements. A second interpretation of the Sermon understands it as a plea for social action and as an ethical treatise which codifies the demands of a social gospel. An interpretation of this kind focuses on the blessing Jesus bestows upon the peacemakers and upon the injunctions to walk the second mile and to give our coats away to those in need. This interpretation is apparently more realistic than the first insofar as it emphasizes the fact that what is best about human nature can never be actualized apart from a diligent attempt to establish a program of social and political reform. A third interpretation, which is perhaps more familiar than the others, regards such a program of social action as utterly unrealistic, suggesting that the Sermon projects an unreachable ideal that attempts to invert the world illegitimately. This unreachable ideal is understood as the expression of a slave mentality and the projection of a wish that the real order should conform to a pattern that we are utterly incapable of establishing by our own power. According to this account, the Sermon on the Mount is simply "platonism for the people" and a deliberate deception designed to turn our attention away from genuine human problems. Finally, a fourth interpretation which is often defended by conservative Biblical scholars is paradoxically related in a positive way to the Nietzschean rejection of the import of the message. According to this account, the Sermon on the Mount depicts an ideal eschatological realm which has nothing to do with the here and now and which has neither social nor political implications for the present situation. Man's essential nature, which might seem to require social action for its complete realization, but which might also be an unreachable ideal is therefore expressed in an eschatological expectation that only God can establish in the real order.

My own interpretation is related to the other alternatives I have mentioned in a variety of ways, but it is also different from them in being essentially theological. In the first place, I defend the view that a proper understanding of the text requires a divine transformation of the human spirit and that it cannot be read properly apart from an acknowledgement of our spiritual bankruptcy. The first words of Jesus in the Sermon are "Blessed are the poor in spirit, for theirs is the kingdom of heaven," implying that an acknowledgement of our poverty and of our need to be transformed is the first condition that the Sermon on the Mount imposes. This means that the Sermon is rooted directly in God and that our essential nature or our social action can neither be actualized nor effected apart from divine power. The Sermon on the Mount is not addressed simply to a universal audience nor to the natural consciousness, but requires a transformation of the spirit before its message can become intelligible. Another way to express this point is to notice that Jesus demands divine perfection from his followers, for the Sermon itself comes to focus in the injunction, "Therefore, be perfect just as your Father in heaven is perfect." However, Jesus never suggests that divine perfection can be achieved by our own action, but only by allowing our lives to be transformed by the kind of perfection that God has already displayed. In this way, the focus of the Sermon is once more God rather than man, requiring a theological interpretation that begins with this primordial fact. Finally, if the perfection to which the Sermon points is to be understood as the expression of divine perfection rather than as a human achievement, the best commentary on it is the theological dimension of other parts of the New Testament that attempt to establish the primacy of the grace of God as standing beyond good and evil. In this book, I have attempted to demonstrate that the Sermon on the Mount is rooted in the perfection of God. As a result, this commentary is theological just insofar as it brings the theological dimension of the other gospels and the epistles to bear upon what might appear to be an essentially ethical, social, or political document.

There can be little question that the Sermon on the Mount has ethical import, or for that matter, that it articulates an ideal that can never be achieved unless the world is inverted. However, the crucial point to notice is that this inversion does not simply point to an eschatological event, but occurs here and now when the admission of a poverty-stricken spirit allows us to enter God's kingdom. When this occurs, we can then become meek and pure in heart, and on this basis, we can begin to undertake the task of reconciliation to which the reference to the peacemaker calls our attention. However, the important theological point to notice is that peace with others presupposes peace with God, and it is finally this presupposition which drives the interpreter of the Sermon on the Mount to give a theological interpretation of its significance.

One of the most crucial theological issues that arises in the Sermon is the contrast between grace and the law, and by implication, the fundamental distinction between the Christian tradition and traditional Judaism. In this connection, it is important to emphasize the fact that Jesus has no intention of repudiating the binding character of the Jewish law, claiming instead that his own teaching is intended to bring the Law and the Prophets to fulfillment. It is true that Matthew represents Jesus as attacking the Pharisees and that on a number of occasions he refers to them as hypocrites. But this does not imply that Jesus is rejecting his origins, or indeed, that every Pharisee is guilty of the kind of legalism that makes the charge of hypocrisy resonate so frequently in the text. It is important to acknowledge the fact that Matthew is concerned to attack excessive legalism as an appropriate response to revelation and that he insists that the only adequate response to the grace of God is a transformed heart. Insofar as the Pharisees insist on the primacy of the Law, and upon a rigid conception of how the Law ought to be interpreted, Jesus criticizes them, pointing instead to a new law that God will one day write upon the heart. As the Christian church was beginning to emerge and to distinguish itself from traditional Judaism, Matthew was no doubt anxious to emphasize the differences between the revolutionary teachings of Jesus and their Jewish origins. However, this does not imply an anti-Semitic attitude, but a quite legitimate concern that the grace of God be recognized as a more primordial conception than the Jewish Law. Insofar as the Pharisees rejected this, Jesus was prepared to repudiate them, yet he did so, not to turn his back on his own people, but in the interest of a new kind of theological relation between God and the world.

Because of the theological focus that unifies my interpretation of the text, and because I assume that the larger Biblical context in which it is rooted is also unified, the methodology of this book differs from the one that is usually employed. Most interpretations of a Biblical text are atomistically philological, generating a hermeneutical standpoint which presupposes that the text is a collection of fragments. There is perhaps a sense in which this is so, but the difficulty with this 19th century approach to Biblical exegesis is that the text is often lost in the attempt to analyze the components and the strata from which the interpreter insists that it has been constructed. In what follows, I have paid careful attention to the original language of the text, but I have also assumed that the Sermon on the Mount has a unity that transcends the fragmentation which it has often been thought to reflect. The Sermon calls our attention to the perfection of God, and I have attempted to show that in the light of this perfection, the text displays a unity which expresses the perfection in which it is grounded. With perfection at the center of the discussion, my own commentary inevitably exhibits philosophical overtones, and indeed, I can scarcely deny that I have come to the theological task I have set myself with philosophical categories and with a traditional philosophical education. However, perhaps the most important thing to say about my approach is that I have written an extended sermon about a Sermon, attempting to embody the perfection of the original message in my own reflections about it. I will be satisfied if the perfection of the original is reflected even dimly in the imperfection of my own response to it, but I am prepared nonetheless to describe this response as a sermon in its own right.

There is a message in the Sermon on the Mount of universal significance, but this universal message can be discovered only in the particularity of the text. The divine perfection which the message attempts to make accessible presupposes that this perfection has been embodied in the Teacher, and the Christ of the Mount is therefore the focal point around which our reflections must turn. We are also unable to begin these reflections without acknowledging our own particularity and without recognizing that a transformation is required of us before we can begin to understand the teachings of Jesus. However, because he is also the universal logos, the words he speaks are relevant to anyone who comes to them from the standpoint of a transformed particularity, and it is these words that finally give us access to a message of universal significance. My own discussion of the Sermon is divided into four parts, beginning with divine perfection and Christian maturity, moving to a discussion of the relation between the past and the future in the light of Jesus' revolutionary teaching, focusing next upon six specific contexts in which divine perfection is expressed, and concluding with some final considerations about the gate, the pathway, and the rock which allows our response to begin, to continue, and to be grounded in God. It is this foundation which gives this commentary a theological orientation and which finally requires it to be a response to a divine interjection.

I would like to express my appreciation to the members of my Sunday School class at the Calvary Baptist Church in State College, Pennsylvania, where this material was first presented. I am also indebted to Mrs. Loretta J. Willits for transcribing the original lessons, for typing the final manuscript, and for helping me supply the references for the completed text. Her work has been invaluable. Finally, I want to express my appreciation and love for my parents, to whom this book is dedicated. They launched me on the path that led to the completion of the manuscript and have encouraged me in developing this rather unusual application of my philosophical education. My father, in particular, will no doubt recognize many of his own words in the text, for I have profited immensely from his sermons about the Gospel of Matthew.

PART I

DIVINE PERFECTION AND CHRISTIAN MATURITY

CHAPTER I

THE CONTEXT OF THE MESSAGE

❦

In the fifth chapter of his gospel Matthew begins his account of the teaching of Jesus by calling our attention to the context in which the Sermon on the Mount was delivered. Most scholars have suggested that the Sermon was not formulated as a unified discourse and that the three chapters in which Matthew presents it represent a collection of sayings uttered on different occasions.[1] If this should prove to be the case, the first two verses of Chapter Five could be regarded as editorial comments intended to serve as an introduction to a series of utterances brought together from a variety of contexts: "And when He saw the multitudes, he went up on the mountain; and after He sat down, His disciples came to Him. And opening His mouth, he began to teach them, saying . . ." (Mt 5.1,2). Whether the Sermon is a continuous discourse or a collection of more episodic utterances, these introductory comments ought not to be ignored, for in making them Matthew generates the framework in which his own presentation of the message of Jesus is to be understood. In doing so, he calls our attention to the kind of audience to which the message of Jesus was directed and points to Jesus himself as the source of his inspiration.

The first verse of Matthew's brief introduction divides into four clauses, and in order to establish a clear conception of the audience to which the Sermon was addressed, it is important to comment on each of them in turn. First, consider "the multitudes." At the beginning of Jesus' Galilean ministry the multitudes thronged him, and he was confronted by a great variety of individuals who were drawn to the initial power of his message. To be sure, the crowds would soon begin to trickle away, and toward the end of his life when he would cry out from the cross, "It is finished" (Jn 19.30), not even all the disciples would be present to hear what he said. At the outset, however, Jesus spoke to multitudes of people, and Matthew records in a series of four episodes the stages that produced the crowds that followed him.

The first of these episodes is found in Chapter Three, where we find a brief account of the preaching of John the Baptist: "Now in those days John the Baptist came, preaching in the wilderness of Judea, saying, 'Repent, for the kingdom of heaven is at hand'" (Mt 3.1,2). When John appeared, both religious leaders and ordinary individuals left Jerusalem to hear this strange and unconventional prophet proclaim his message of repentance and of the kingdom of God. However, from the perspective of the gospel writers, John's ultimate purpose was to be the forerunner of Christ, and John himself makes this clear by claiming that another messenger is coming who is greater than he. The crowds that followed Jesus in the early stages of his ministry can thus be traced to the original witness of John, for it was John the Baptist who pointed forward so persistently to the one who was coming.

The second stage of this developing account if to be found at the end of Chapter Three, where Jesus comes to meet John beside the river to be baptized.

> Then Jesus arrived from Galilee at the Jordan coming to John, to be baptized by him. But John tried to prevent Him, saying, "I have need to be baptized of You, and do You come to me?" But Jesus answering said to him, "Permit it at this time; for in this way it is fitting for us to fulfill all righteousness." Then he permitted Him. And after being baptized, Jesus went up immediately from the water; and behold, the heavens were opened, and he saw the Spirit of God descending as a dove, and coming upon Him, and behold, a voice out of the heavens, saying, "This is My Beloved Son, in whom I am well-pleased" (Mt 3.13–17).

The crowds that followed John saw the baptism of Jesus, participating in this way in the inaugural moment of Jesus' own ministry.

But what does Jesus do after his baptism? He does not plunge immediately into the furor of activity in which he is soon to be immersed. Instead, he goes out into the desert for forty days to be tempted by the devil. During those forty days, Jesus confronts a crucial question in solitude, in hunger, and in thirst: "When I go back to the people, what will be the guiding thread of my teaching and the central content of my message?" But what were the temptations Jesus faced as they have a bearing on the answer he gave? All three temptations pointed to possibilities Jesus could have embraced but from which he turned away: "Turn these stones into bread and feed the multitudes, and you can be assured that they will follow you"; "Fall down and worship me, and I will put you in charge of the political order so that your kingdom will come in sociopolitical terms"; "Go up onto the pinnacle of the Temple and plunge down, and when the people see that you are unharmed, they will gladly follow you" (Mt 4.3–10). Yet each time Jesus turns away, and he does so because during those forty days he is coming to a crystalized formulation of a richer teaching.

Finally, at the end of Chapter Four we find a fourth episode which leads directly into the opening verse of Matthew's introductory comments. In Chapter Four Matthew says:

> And Jesus was going about in all Galilee, teaching in their synagogues, and proclaiming the gospel of the kingdom, and healing every kind of disease and every kind of sickness among the people. And the news about Him went out into all Syria; and they brought to Him all who were ill, taken with various diseases and pains, demoniacs, epileptics, paralytics; and He healed them. And great multitudes followed Him from Galilee and Decapolis and Jerusalem and Judea and from beyond the Jordan (Mt 4.23–25).

This last verse summarizes the geography of Palestine, and it comes to focus in the assertion that the multitudes referred to at the beginning of Chapter Five come from all the separate political subdivisions of the entire region to follow Jesus. Thus Matthew begins Chapter Five with the phrase, "And when He saw the multitudes" (Mt 5.1).

But notice what Jesus does in the second clause of Matthew's brief introduction: He goes up onto a mountain, or more accurately, up the hillside. At this point most commentators suggest that Matthew's gospel intends to remind us of the earlier Old Testament tradition, and more specifically, of the first covenant that was ratified in the formulation of the Ten Commandments. Moses went up onto a mountain where the first covenant came to focus in the first Law. Matthew, writing with Hebrew apologetic purposes in view, wishes to remind us of this fact, and thus he sketches a picture of Jesus going up onto a hillside to begin his teaching.[2] However, this time what is at stake is a new covenant; on this occasion, what is involved is a new Law; in this context, what Jesus formulates is the Law the prophet Jeremiah mentions when he says: "One day I will write a new law on your hearts" (Jer 31.33).

Having considered the multitudes, and having noticed that Jesus goes up the hillside, what are we to say about the third phrase, "and He sat down"? Rabbis always taught sitting down, and that is how Jesus taught on this occasion. However, the fact that he sat down reflects the more fundamental fact that he was perfectly relaxed and that his fundamental intention was to teach within this framework. The hysteria of the crowds was mounting to almost incalculable proportions; Jesus would have to face that hysteria on subsequent occasions; and at the end of his ministry, it would come to a climax when he would ride into Jerusalem and the people who had been expecting the long-awaited Messiah would shout, "Save us now! Bring salvation now!" (Mt 21.9). But at this point, Jesus begins to address his audience simply by sitting down and teaching. However, we shall also find that if we listen to the message of Jesus, the excitement expressed externally by the crowd will emerge at a much more profound level from the center of his teaching.

Finally, consider the fact that "His disciples came to Him." His followers were devoutly religious, but they were not the depersonalized, idealistic apostles often represented in stained glass windows. Quite to the contrary, they were ordinary men, living in occupied territory and no doubt resentful of the Roman occupation. They also had a host of alternatives about how to respond to their religious and political predicaments. They observed the Pharisees, steeped in tradition and concerned above all else to obey the Law, and that alternative surely occurred to them, devout as they were. They saw the Sadducees, much more liberal, believing very little, but at least wealthy and able to function in some measure of ease in occupied territory. Surely some of them must have considered that possibility. And they heard the rabble and the rumblings in the streets and were no doubt tempted to join the Zealots who had decided to deal with their political predicament in revolutionary terms. The disciples who came to Jesus did not live in a cultural or political vacuum, but confronted him distressed about their circumstances.[3] Nevertheless, Jesus had called them a few days or weeks before, and they had decided to follow him. And now the crucial question becomes: what is the distinctive message the Teacher wishes to convey to his followers?

Notice also that when the disciples approach Jesus, *a space opens up* between Jesus and the disciples on the one hand, and the crowd on the other. Matthew begins Chapter Five with the multitudes, and he begins in this way because Jesus was confronted by countless individuals who were drawn to the power of his preaching and to the mighty acts he performed. However, the striking fact about the Sermon is that it can only begin when he leaves the multitudes behind, goes up a hillside, and generates a space between himself and the multitudes who were crowding in upon him. Moreover, the Sermon does not commence until his disciples are willing to come across the space that Jesus opens up to listen to his teaching. When the disciples first encounter Jesus, they are no doubt dimly aware of the vast difference between his absolute perfection and their own degenerate condition. Nevertheless, they find that he is willing to teach them only if they make an initial commitment.

At the most fundamental level, we have a clear indication in this verse of the kind of response Jesus demands from his followers. We come in multitudes—for whatever reason—attracted by the words and by the witness of Jesus. For that particular crowd, there might have been something attractive in Jesus' appearance, or about what he said, or about the tremendous power that was to be found in him. Hope for a new world was no doubt generated simply by being in his presence. Yet it is absolutely crucial to see that Jesus, knowing what he could have done with the multitudes in the light of the tremendous power he exercised, turns *away* from them, lets a space open up between himself and them, permits a few disciples to come across that space, and having had a positive response from a small group of men, begins to teach them in the calmest and most deliberate fashion imaginable. As we will discover when we reach the end of Chapter Seven, the crowd begins to move forward as the Sermon progresses so that the seventh chapter ends with the phrase, "and the crowds were amazed at His teaching, for He taught them as one having authority, and not as their scribes" (Mt 7.28,29). At the beginning of Chapter Five, there is a space; at the end of Chapter Seven, the multitudes reappear; and in between, we find the Sermon itself which was addressed initially to Jesus' closest followers. However, what is most important to notice is that an initial moment of separation must occur if we are to hear the message of Jesus, and that only if we choose to cross the chasm that separates us from him will the words he speaks be able to address our fragmented condition.

But what shall we say about verse two, where Matthew concludes his brief introduction by claiming, "And opening His mouth He began to teach them, saying . . ." (Mt 5.2)? The phrase itself is redundant, and there can be little doubt that the other gospel writers would have been much more economical. For example, Mark's gospel depicts Jesus in action and is a breathlessly written document, one event tumbling after the other with scarcely a pause in between. By contrast, Matthew is more expansive, interlacing sayings of Jesus with the activities in which he was engaged by using phrases of the kind before us. Yet whatever Matthew's intentions, we can perhaps find a deeper significance in the expansive form he chooses to adopt. There are other ways to teach besides opening one's mouth. One teaches by who one is; one teaches by what one does; and one teaches by what one says. Moreover, it is important to notice that Jesus teaches in all three ways at once and that he is able to do this because as the writer of the Gospel of John would later formulate the point, he is himself the Living Word (Jn 1.14). In the Sermon on the Mount, Jesus is able to teach his disciples because he is the Living

Logos, and this fact expresses itself not only in what he says, but also in who he is and in what he does.

One of the finest books written about this Sermon is entitled *The Christ of the Mount,* and it bears this title because the author realizes that the words spoken in the Sermon are rooted in the 'being' of the one who speaks.[4] In this book, E. Stanley Jones calls our attention to three aspects of Jesus' relationship with the Father that causes his Sermon to have the ring of authority and authenticity about it. In the first place, he suggests that the Word of God is the *specification of God in accessible form.* Of course, Jesus claims to be one with the Father, and we begin our own discussion with this presupposition. But the importance of the incarnation is that when Jesus reveals the Father, the Father receives *specification in a finite form that he would not otherwise have.* In John's gospel Jesus says that no one has seen the Father at any time and that he alone has manifested him to us (Jn 6.46, 10.30). Thus, the Living Word that appears on the mountain is the specification of God in accessible form. In the second place, Stanley Jones suggests that the Word of God that Jesus expresses is also the *simplification of God.* In the *Republic,* Plato tells us that he wishes to sketch a picture of the human soul, and he says that since the best way to do this is to draw a picture written large, he will turn away from speaking about the soul to speaking about the city. Thus Plato suggests that if we can see the larger picture of the city, perhaps we can also learn something about the structure of the soul.[5] By analogy, when Jesus speaks to his followers, he both specifies God and simplifies him, and he simplifies him by making him accessible in human terms. Finally, the author suggests that the one who sits on the mountain and who intends to teach his disciples is *the pathway that leads us to the Father.*[6] In John's gospel Jesus says, "I am the way, and the truth, and the life; no one comes to the Father, but through Me" (Jn 14.6). That is the dogmatic foundation upon which the Christian tradition rests. There are many dialogues that can and should occur between one religion and another, but the foundation of the Christian faith is expressed in the sentence uttered by Jesus himself that stands behind his teaching: "I am the pathway that will lead you to the Father; I am the truth that will reveal what is original and that will never degenerate into counterfeit coin; and I am the source of Life and am the Light in which the truth I have come to reveal will become visible."

Before we plunge into the Sermon in detail, let us finally ask the crucial question about the content of the message Jesus intends to convey to his followers. What is the focus of the Sermon on the Mount? What is its center? What does the whole thing mean? In the book to which I have just referred, the author suggests that the focal point of the Sermon is to be found in the last verse of the fifth chapter of Matthew where Jesus says, "Therefore you are to be perfect as your Father in heaven is perfect"[7] (Mt 5.48). By contrast with this demand, the writer reminds us that other religions promise many things. Some promise justice, for as the Hebrew prophet Amos says, "Let justice roll down like the rivers, and righteousness like a mighty stream" (Am 5.24). Others promise pleasure, for as popular accounts of Islam suggest, it finally comes to focus there. Some promise nothingness; others promise divinity; and still others promise progress. What, by contrast, does Jesus insist upon and not just promise, but demand? The crucial sentence is an imperative. It says: "Be perfect!" And it concludes by suggesting that the perfection Jesus has in mind is not simply human, but is in fact divine.[8] Yet at this point the question arises, "How can this be?!" Even the Scriptures themselves raise serious questions about how perfection can ever be achieved. For example, Isaiah says that our righteousness is like filthy rags when it is compared with the righteousness of God (Is 64.6); the Psalmist claims that there is none righteous, no not one (Ps 14.1); and in an even more familiar passage the Apostle Paul tells us that all have sinned and fallen short of God's absolute perfection (Rom 3.23). How then can the focal point of the Sermon on the Mount be a sentence that says, "Be perfect"? And be perfect "just as God is perfect"?

In responding to these questions, it is important to focus on the Greek word that is translated "perfection" in this passage. The word *telios* is the term from which we get the word *telos,* or "end." As a result, the word translated "perfection" means the end toward which a developing being is oriented so that when it reaches that end, it will finally be mature, and by implication, be what it was meant to become. The universe about which Jesus spoke was not the mechanical universe of matter in motion and the clangor of machines, but was instead a world understood in terms of purposes, ends, and goals. As a result, the crucial question to be asked about a person or a thing was not a question about its internal constitution, but the more fundamental question about what that thing or person was meant to be. In the passage before us, Jesus formulates this fundamental question by using the term *telios,* which can be translated with the English word "perfection," but which can perhaps be rendered more adequately in terms of the concept of maturity. "Be engaged," Jesus says, "in the task of becoming what you were meant to be, reaching the *telos,* the purpose, the goal, and the maturity for which you were intended." In these terms, the Sermon on the Mount intends to bring the followers of Jesus into a kingdom that has both come and is coming and into a way of life that makes it possible for us to live in terms of the end toward which we ought to be directed. As a result, what is about to unfold in this message is an account of what life in God's kingdom should be, directed as it is toward enabling the follower of Jesus to become what he was meant to be.

Perhaps Paul speaks most clearly for the kind of follower Jesus has in mind when he says in the third chapter of Philippians:

> Not that I have already obtained it, or have already become perfect, but I press on in order that I may lay hold of that for which also I was laid hold of by Christ Jesus. Brethren, I do not regard myself as having laid hold of it yet; but one thing I do: forgetting what lies behind and reaching forward to what lies ahead, I press on toward the goal for the prize of the upward call of God in Christ Jesus (Phil 3.12–14).

In these sentences, the center of the Sermon on the Mount comes to focus, and we are confronted not only with the goal of Christian maturity, but also with the kind of response Jesus demands in our own case.

CHAPTER II

ENTRANCE INTO GOD'S KINGDOM

❦

In establishing the context for the Sermon on the Mount, Matthew mentions the multitudes, refers to a mountain, and says that after Jesus sat down upon it, his disciples came to him (Mt 5.1). And when the space opens up between the surrounding crowds and the disciples close at hand, Matthew adds that "opening His mouth He began to teach them, saying . . ." (Mt 5.2). Before we turn to the content of the Sermon, it is important to notice a striking fact about the tenses of the verbs in these first two verses. Every verb but the last is in the aorist tense, which means that the verbs in question point to *specific moments in time*. At a specific moment he saw the multitudes; at a subsequent moment, he went up onto a mountain; subsequently, he sat down; and at still another moment, his disciples came to him. Thus Matthew records four momentary occurrences, each in sequence. However, the last verb of Matthew's introductory comments is in the imperfect tense; it is translated in our text "and He began to teach them"; but one of the possible implications of the Greek imperfect in this case is that he not only began to teach for a period of time, but also repeated himself often enough for his audience to understand his intentions. It is very unlikely that the complex content of the Sermon on the Mount was formulated only once, and as a result, we should perhaps imagine four momentary events followed by a stretched out sequence of other events in which Jesus repeats more than once the essential content of his teaching. In any case, it is this essential content upon which we must focus our attention.

The first and most familiar section of the Sermon on the Mount is to be found in verses three through twelve of Chapter Five and is called "the Beatitudes" (Mt 5.3–12). The Beatitudes, of course, are blessings, and the word "blessed" therefore serves to bracket the entire initial segment of Jesus' teaching. As a result, the first question that arises should focus on the meaning of this crucial expression and upon the significance of the brackets it places around the nine Beatitudes to be found at the beginning of the message. It is important to remember that the word "blessed" has a long and venerable history in the Hebrew tradition. In addition to the Law, the Old Testament records a number of blessings and in fact includes a collection of sayings that can be classified as "Blessings and Cursings." For example, in the first verse of the first Psalm, the Psalmist declares: "Blessed is the man who walketh not in the counsel of the ungodly, nor standeth in the way of sinners, nor sitteth in the seat of the scornful" (Ps 1.1). This is a beatitude, or a blessing, and it is this kind of traditional context that the blessings Jesus bestows upon his disciples presuppose. It is also a familiar fact that the Patriarchs of the Old Testament often sought the blessings both of God and of their parents. For example, Jacob was even willing to become a trickster in order to receive his father's blessing, and he was willing to do this because the blessing of his father was the expression in human terms of what it means to stand in a relationship with God that brings blessedness to the human soul (Gn 27). Thus, when Jesus begins to teach his disciples, he introduces the content of his message with a word that resonates with the past history and with the recollective consciousness of his audience.

It is also important to notice that the word Jesus introduces at the outset points to the concept of happiness. There are two words for happiness in Greek that our author could have used. One is the word *eudaimonia* and is the term Aristotle uses when he speaks about human happiness in the *Nicomachean Ethics*.[1] By contrast, Matthew uses the word *makarios,* which points beyond human happiness to a divine realm and to the kind of happiness appropriate to it. All the Beatitudes begin with a reference to the divine happiness that Jesus intends to make accessible to his followers when they become citizens of God's kingdom. However, in using this word, Jesus not only points to divine happiness, but calls our attention to a relational fact as well. In the original use of the word, a relation was always implied between the one who possessed divine happiness and the benefactor who brought it. In this case, one receives a gift and is divinely happy, and divine happiness results from the relation he bears to the gift giver.[2] Aristotle claims that human happiness is the activity of the soul in accord with what we were meant to be, and the implication is that happiness results from human activity that reflects what is best about our own nature.[3] By contrast, in speaking about divine happiness Jesus suggests that it results, not from the unfolding of our nature, but from the transformation of it through a gift that comes from God. Thus, the happiness Jesus mentions here is not something we grow into; it is not the expression of our own self-development; it is not a matter of reaching for the heights or of finding happiness because we have accomplished the end for which we were intended. Quite to the contrary, the blessings in this case are divine because they come as a gift and because they are made accessible to us through a relation in which we stand to the sustaining ground of life itself.

Finally, the concept of happiness in question here is not simply divine and is not merely relational, but is also a deeply inner condition. On more than one occasion Jesus claims that his kingdom has already come and that this kingdom is to be found within. But Jesus also suggests that the inner condition he has come to bring is accessible to us no matter what the external circumstances.[4] This is the most paradoxical dimension of what Jesus has in mind when he refers to divine happiness. It is tempting to understand happiness in cyclical terms and to identify it with a positive convergence of inner feeling and external circumstances that allows us to achieve the fulfillment we seek. By contrast, Jesus suggests that the kind of happiness he brings is an inner condition that can be achieved regardless of the circumstances in which we find ourselves. Jesus is attempting to break the cyclical pattern of natural existence, and he is calling his followers to a way of life in which one can find divine happiness even in the midst of discord. The fundamental task of human existence is to reach the place where this can be true of us, so that when calamities come, we not only face them by girding ourselves up to do so, but also confront them in the light of our absolute assurance that we stand at the center of God's perfect peace. It is this perfect peace, made accessible as a divine gift and as an inner condition that can be achieved regardless of circumstances, to which the Beatitudes are intended to call our attention.

As we turn to the Beatitudes themselves, it is important to notice that there are two versions of the Sermon in which they occur, one of which is to be found in Chapters Five through Seven of Matthew's gospel, and the other of which is recorded in the sixth chapter of Luke, verses twelve through forty-nine. In addition, there are nine Beatitudes in Matthew's account and only four in Luke's, and in each case, there are important differences between the two versions that must be considered as we proceed with our more detailed discussion. In fact, the first Beatitude to be found in Matthew's gospel has a counterpart in Luke which is by no means identical with it. Matthew says, "Blessed are the poor in spirit, for theirs is the kingdom of heaven" (Mt 5.3), while Luke says simply, "Blessed are the poor, for yours is the kingdom of God" (Lk 6.20). Now if the one being addressed is poor, the natural response is that Luke's more direct and primitive formulation is correct, while if the one who listens is rich, he would of course be inclined to prefer the version to be found in Matthew.[5] However, the real problem is that if we approach the text from either point of view, we will miss the target. The preference for Luke or the preference for Matthew comes to focus on the one who expresses the preference, while the whole point of the Sermon on the Mount is to call our attention away from ourselves to the gift-giver from whom divine happiness can be received.

One of the best commentaries on this first Beatitude as Matthew expresses it is in fact to be found in the eighteenth chapter of Luke, verses ten through fourteen:

> Two men went up into the temple to pray, one a Pharisee, and the other a tax-gatherer. The Pharisee stood and was praying thus to himself, "God, I thank Thee that I am not like other people: swindlers, unjust, adulterers, or even like this tax-gatherer. I fast twice a week, I pay tithes of all that I get." But the tax-gatherer, standing

some distance away, was even unwilling to lift up his eyes to
heaven, but was beating his breast, saying, "God, be merciful to
me, the sinner!" I tell you, this man went down to his house
justified rather than the other; for everyone who exalts himself
shall be humbled, but he who humbles himself shall be exalted (Lk
18.10–14).

Notice that in Luke's story it is the tax-gatherer who is rich, not
poor, and that it is the religious leader standing in such radical contrast with him who is most likely poor.[6] Yet when they both pray,
only the tax-gatherer goes down to his house justified, not because
he is rich, nor because he is poor, but because he recognizes that he is
spiritually bankrupt. In his prayer the tax-gatherer says, "Lord, be
merciful to me, the sinner." When one prays that prayer, all the rest
of the world drops away; and whether rich or poor, one comes face
to face with his bankrupt condition, an acknowledgment of which is
the first step in becoming a member of God's kingdom.

The word for "poor" in this verse is *ptochos,* and the implication
of the word is that the person in question is aware of his condition
and that he makes a self-conscious appraisal and acknowledgment of
it. So Jesus says, "Blessed are the poor in spirit," or in a more
expansive form, "divinely happy is the one who acknowledges his
spiritual poverty and his bankruptcy self-consciously, for his is the
kingdom of heaven." But why does Jesus focus on the concept of
spirit in this first Beatitude? Does he merely intend to spiritualize
what could be stated more straightforwardly and economically, or
does his choice of this conception express a more fundamental intention? Perhaps we can begin to answer this question by noticing that
four words are used in the New Testament to characterize the human
being. The Scriptures speak about the mind; they speak about the
body; they speak about the soul; and they speak about the spirit.
Presumably, the soul is not only the unity of mental and physical
dimensions, but also has life, which can be understood as a dynamically developing spirit that sustains every genuinely human act and
which generates the surging power that expresses itself in every
instance of human greatness. But what does the spirit do when it is
left to its own devices? It attempts to drive to what lies beyond; it

reaches up to what is higher; it attempts to scale the heights; and when it is taken to its logical conclusion, it finally demands that God relinquish his throne so that it can sit there in his place.

There is something absolutely indispensable about the spiritual dimension of human existence. Without it, we would be impoverished; without it, we would never move from stage to stage; without it, we would never develop toward what lies beyond our original condition. However, the tragedy of the human spirit is that it often storms the gates and seeks to reach the heights out of its own resources, making access to divine happiness a distinctively human achievement. But what does Jesus say when he addresses his disciples? "Divinely happy, relationally happy, happy as an inner condition is the one who acknowledges that he is poor in spirit, and that spirit in the merely human sense is utterly bankrupt." Thus he suggests that no matter how persistently we reach beyond the human realm to scale the heights, we will never be able to do so as an expression of an unregenerated spirit. Formulated in somewhat different terms, the Sermon on the Mount begins by presupposing what John later describes as the new birth (Jn 3.7). It is not a collection of ethical principles designed to organize the world in merely humanistic terms. Quite to the contrary, the first Beatitude is intended to formulate the condition for entrance into God's kingdom, and the only condition is that one acknowledge that he is spiritually bankrupt and say with the tax-gatherer, "Lord, be merciful to me, the sinner." Moreover, Jesus says that the moment we make this admission, we will inherit the kingdom of heaven. This first Beatitude, then, expresses a single condition that leads us into a new kind of family and into a new kind of citizenship within the kingdom of God.

The phrase, "the kingdom of heaven," occurs repeatedly in Matthew. The Hebrew audience would never use the word "God" directly, so they relied upon a circumlocution. Instead of "Yahweh" they said "Adonai" and hence "Lord" instead of "God." In a similar way, instead of saying "the kingdom of God," they said in a circumlocution, "the kingdom of heaven." We can thus say the same thing more directly and in a form that reflects the content of our earlier

analysis in the following way: "Divinely happy because of a relationship is the one who acknowledges his own poverty of spirit, knowing that the human being left to himself is bankrupt; for the moment
one acknowledges this fact, he can become a citizen of God's kingdom."

One further way to formulate this point is to suggest that if we
are to enter God's kingdom, it is necessary that we empty ourselves,
or perhaps more accurately, that we acknowledge that we are empty
already. The act of self-emptying is an act that results from our prior
recognition of the fact that we *are* empty. When we say, "I am empty,
I am poverty-stricken, I am bankrupt," there are no doubt a host of
reservations behind our backs. Yet what God requires is not that we
empty ourselves so that those reservations vanish, but that we acknowledge our emptiness, whatever our reservations may be. It is
only when we embrace our spiritual poverty that we can come to
stand in a relation with God that brings fullness out of emptiness.
And if we do so, the self-emptying that follows in the other Beatitudes will merely become a reflection of the first act that says, "Lord,
I am empty already; be merciful to me a sinner."

What shall we say when we turn to the second Beatitude with
this concept of emptiness clearly in mind? Again we find the word
"blessed" with the same connotations: divine happiness, relational
happiness, inner happiness regardless of circumstances characterizes
the one who is about to be described. But notice also the specific
content of verse four: "Blessed are those who mourn, for they shall
be comforted" (Mt 5.4). How is mourning related to our being poor
in spirit and to our entrance into God's kingdom? What does mourning have to do with acknowledging our emptiness in virtue of which
the kingdom of God has already been made our possession? What
occurs after that paradoxical moment when emptiness becomes fullness and when the zero point of poverty becomes the overflowing
abundance of God's infinite richness? What always happens after one
has been to the mountain top is that he comes down the other side.
Never expect to have that first moment without having the second.
And Matthew, reporting the words of Jesus, comes to that second
moment when he says, "Having entered God's kingdom, and having

gone to the mountain top of fullness which displaces your emptiness, mourning always comes."

What is the source of the mourning? In his epistles, Paul speaks about the source of mourning by using the word "tribulation" (Rom 5.3). After one enters God's kingdom, he finds that the buffeting begins. It sometimes comes from the outside; it sometimes comes from within; but in either case, it is at this point that the struggle involved in human experience is to be located. Thus, while the first Beatitude formulates the condition for entering God's kingdom, the second focuses our attention upon the discord, the difficulty, and the tribulation that follows inevitably, both from outside and from within. But Jesus says, "Blessed not only are the ones who acknowledge that they are bankrupt, but also the ones who, on the next morning or the next, face the discord of tribulation."

The buffeting we experience and the mourning that accompanies it sometimes have their source in the re-emergence of our sinful nature. It is absolutely impossible to scale the heights even though we are citizens of the heights! Yet we persistently attempt to do so out of our own resources and driven by the power of our own spirit. The human spirit left to itself has a double role: it is active at the start; it is canceled when we acknowledge our spiritual poverty; but it re-emerges in our struggle with what the classical theologians called "our old sinful nature."[7] As a result, the mourning which we must confront sometimes comes from the buffeting within, produced by the struggle of the soul with itself as it attempts to re-embrace its natural condition.

There is a second dimension of the concept of mourning that must also be considered. When I enter God's kingdom, I mourn not only for myself, but also when I look beyond my own experience toward the surrounding world. Those who see ethical implications in the Sermon on the Mount are clearly correct when they suggest that this is not a sermon intended only for the isolated religious consciousness, but a message that also puts us in touch with the larger world. We often mourn on the inside only to forget about the groanings of the rest of the world. Of course, the recognition of the larger world does not cancel our own groanings, nor overcome the predicament that results from the re-emergence of our sinful nature. However, it does put us in touch with a wider context and allows us to recognize the fact that the whole creation is groaning along with us as we continue to struggle with our fragmented condition (Rom 8.22). Jesus calls our attention to both these dimensions when he speaks about the mourning consciousness and when he says that in the midst of our groanings, we will be comforted.

What is the source of comfort to which Jesus refers at this juncture? Before he was about to leave his disciples, Jesus said in the fourteenth chapter of John, "And I will send you another comforter, and that other comforter will dwell within" (Jn 14.16,17). The scriptures as a whole are remarkably consistent. In John, Jesus speaks about the Spirit as a comforter. Here he says that those who are poor in spirit and those who mourn under the impact of their own groaning and of the groaning of the larger world will be comforted. If we bring these two references together we can see that the comfort he intends in both instances is the comfort that the Divine Spirit will bring the troubled spirit, sometimes torn apart by the tribulation it must confront. Thus Jesus says, "Blessed are those who acknowledge their bankrupt condition," and having done that, "Blessed are those who mourn both on the inside and on the outside," for the Comforter that Jesus sends will bring comfort to the fragmented soul.

Finally, what shall we say about the third Beatitude to be found in verse five? "Blessed are the meek, for they shall inherit the earth" (Mt 5.5). How many people would love to be meek in this sense, and how many would despise meekness in this same sense?[8] And of course, how many have already despised it? But what does the word "meekness" mean within this context? There are two other words that we could use: one is "humble" and the other is "gentle." Perhaps the word "gentle" is a better translation. "Meekness" may very well have degenerated to a point beyond redemption. For a contemporary audience, perhaps the verse should be translated, "Blessed are the gentle, for they shall inherit the earth."

But before we re-translate the term, let us return briefly to the word "meekness." There are only two individuals in the entire scriptural tradition who are called meek: the first is Moses and the second is Christ. Moses, who stands at the foundation of the Old Testament community, and who leads two million people on the long journey from bondage to freedom; Moses, who has the courage to go back home when he does not know how to unravel the strands of his tangled origins; Moses, who stands before Pharoah and says in thundering terms, "Let my people go!" (Ex 5.1)—this same Moses is described in the Scriptures as meek. And Jesus, often caricatured for his meekness, but who works for years in the carpenter's shop, not in order to become weak, but to become strong; Jesus, who stands before Pilate and refuses to reply; Jesus, who goes to the cross having said to the disciples, "No one takes my life away. I lay it down, and I will take it up again." (Jn 10.18)—he is one who is also described as meek, as humble, and as gentle.

Now Jesus uses this same word when he says, "Blessed are the meek, for they shall inherit the earth." Where does gentleness come from when it appears? Let me suggest that it comes from the intersection of the empty self and the mourning self;[9] from the identity of the self that has confessed its bankruptcy with the self that has been buffeted by extreme tribulation; and from the unity of the self that mourns with the self that has caught a glimpse of the groaning world to which it responds. It is when one stands at all those other places that he can sometimes reach that richer place where his life can be described as gentle. The richest acts of gentleness are the acts that come not only from strength, but also from one who being strong, becomes weak; who, having become weak, carries not only his own burdens but also the burdens of the world; and who finally, out of the intersection of those other characteristics, reaches out toward another person in the meek, the humble, and the gentle act.

There is a developmental dimension in these first three Beatitudes: the empty self, and the mourning self that reaches beyond its own emptiness to the groaning of the larger world becomes, in the third place and in its highest manifestation, the gentle self. But notice also that Jesus says that the gentle shall inherit the earth. The first Beatitude says that the poor in spirit shall inherit the kingdom of heaven; the second Beatitude brings this kingdom within and points to the Comforter who will one day come; while the third Beatitude brings these two dimensions together by asserting: "You will not only inherit the heavenly region, and you will not only be comforted within, but you will also be able to inherit the earth." So there is no place—height or depth, outside or inside—that falls outside the blessings that Jesus wishes to bestow upon his followers. And there is no limit to the inheritance, for that final inheritance reaches up to heaven, pulls heaven down and places it within, and lets the inside reach out to everything that lies beyond, inheriting the larger world.

John describes the inheritance Jesus has in mind, and the radical transformation it will finally produce, in the twenty-first chapter of Revelation, verses one through seven:

> And I saw a new heaven and a new earth; for the first heaven and the first earth were passed away, and there was no longer any sea. And I saw the holy city, new Jerusalem, coming down out of heaven from God, made ready as a bride adorned for her husband. And I heard a loud voice from the throne, saying, "Behold, the tabernacle of God is among men, and He shall dwell among them, and they shall be His people, and God Himself shall be among them, and He shall wipe away every tear from their eyes; and there shall no longer be any death; there shall no longer be any mourning, or crying, or pain; the first things have passed away." And He who sits on the throne said, "Behold, I am making all things new." And He said to me, "It is done. I am the Alpha and the Omega, the beginning and the end. I will give to the one who thirsts from the spring of the water of life without cost. *He who overcomes shall inherit these things, and I will be his God and he will be My Son*" (Rv 21.1–7).

CHAPTER III

THE OUTWARD JOURNEY

The first three Beatitudes are addressed to the poor in spirit, to those that mourn, and to the meek or gentle consciousness that brings these two dimensions together in a unity that produces a divine inheritance. In these verses Jesus reaches up to the heights and gives us access to the kingdom of heaven; he reaches down to the center of our being and brings comfort in the midst of tribulation; and he reaches out to the rim of the world to give us a divine inheritance that will one day express itself in the real order. The audience Jesus addressed was interested in the concept of an inheritance, not only because of the structure of their religious tradition, but because they had been promised a land that stretched from Dan to Beersheba and from the valley of the Tigris and Euphrates to the Mediterranean Sea. Thus Jesus responds to their expectations when he claims that they can inherit the earth if they move from poverty of spirit, to the mourning consciousness, to a gentleness of soul that can reach out beyond its fragmented condition to embrace a larger world.

In the next three Beatitudes, Jesus begins to develop the outward thrust of his message, and he does so in an especially striking fashion in verse six by claiming: "Blessed are those who hunger and thirst for righteousness, for they shall be satisfied" (Mt 5.6). It has often been suggested that hungering and thirsting are the most fundamental human cravings and that Jesus taps something deeply embedded in our consciousness when he speaks in these terms.[1] However, it is also important to notice that the reference to hungering and thirsting is expressed in the text in present active participles, which in Greek denote activities that occur continuously. In English the present tense usually refers to a particular moment in time, but in this case, the participles suggest continuous action, not only occurring now, but also stretching out into the future. Thus, verse six should be rendered, "Blessed are those who keep on hungering and thirsting for righteousness, for they will be satisfied."

We should also notice that the word "righteousness" in the Greek text is preceded by the definite article, which is usually left untranslated in our English versions. To be true to the text, perhaps we should include it and re-translate the entire sentence as follows: "Blessed are those who keep on hungering and thirsting for *the* righteousness, for they will be satisfied." But what is the righteousness in question? If I have understood the Sermon on the Mount correctly, it is not righteousness in general; not your righteousness or mine; but the only kind of righteousness worth having, which is of course the righteousness of God. Jesus wishes to bestow divine happiness upon his followers, but as the first Beatitude suggests, happiness of this kind becomes accessible only if we renounce the kind of righteousness that results from human achievement. Thus, Jesus says to those who are renounced in spirit, "Blessed are those who hunger and thirst after God's righteousness, for they shall be filled."

What does the word "righteousness" mean in the New Testament? The most adequate account is to be found in the third chapter of Romans, where Paul begins his theological formulation of the message of Jesus. Some scholars have suggested that a chasm separates the teachings of Jesus from the later reflections of Paul, as though Paul the theologian distorted what Jesus had expressed with such paradoxical clarity.[2] By contrast, I am confident that the interpretation of the concept of righteousness in Paul's Epistle to the Romans can give us access to what Jesus himself means when he speaks about righteousness in the text before us. With this assumption in mind, let us turn then to verses nine through twelve of the third chapter of Romans, where Paul says:

> What then? Are we better than they? Not at all; for we have already charged that both Jews and Greeks are all under sin; as it is

written, "There is none righteous, not even one; there is none who
understands, there is none who seeks for God; all have turned
aside, together they have become useless; there is none who does
good; there is not even one" (Rom 3.9–12).

The first kind of righteousness to which Paul refers is the righteousness we achieve when we are left to ourselves, and he suggests
that this kind of righteousness is utterly worthless as a way of gaining entrance into God's kingdom. God's response is that human
righteousness is absolutely inadequate and that because of its merely
human origins, it can only be regarded as filthy rags. And since Jesus
himself has already suggested that the human spirit is unable to attain
the happiness it seeks by developing its own capacities, we can conclude that the righteousness for which we should hunger and thirst is
not a righteousness of our own making, nor one that is accessible in
human terms alone.

But how does Paul continue his argument in the familiar words of
Romans 3:23? There he says simply, "For all have sinned and fall short
of the glory of God" (Rom 3.23). In this verse the word "glory" means
"perfection," and by implication, it calls our attention away from
ourselves to the righteousness of God. Or in terms more appropriate
to the Sermon on the Mount, the perfection we are asked to embrace is
divine rather than human and becomes accessible to us, not as the
result of human achievement, but simply as a divine gift. Yet how is
this divine gift to be obtained? Paul responds to this question in verse
twenty-four of the third chapter of Romans by claiming that those
who have fallen short of God's glory have been "justified as a gift by
His grace" and that God did this so that he might demonstrate his
righteousness and so that he might be both "just and the justifier of the
one who has faith in Jesus" (Rom 3.24–26).

It should go without saying that an adequate explication of this
passage is a difficult theological task, and it might seem that the
intricate theological position being developed here has little relevance
to the straightforward reference of Jesus to the concept of righteousness in Beatitude Four. However, let us simply notice the most crucial element of Paul's intentions as it has a bearing on the earlier
teaching of Jesus. Paul claims that our righteousness is utterly worthless; that God's righteousness is absolutely perfect; and that there is

no logical or dialectical connection between them. However, he also says that the one who is just chooses to become the justifier, and that when he does this, we have a third sense of righteousness which reaches across the chasm that separates the first two and which is simply given as a gift. The concept of righteousness therefore stands before us in a threefold guise: the worthless righteousness of our own; the perfect righteousness of God; and that perfect righteousness made accessible to us as a gift in the One who addresses us on the hillside. It is my positive if somewhat unorthodox suggestion that it is a gift of this kind which allows the divine happiness mentioned repeatedly in the Sermon on the Mount to be bestowed upon us and which gives us our initial access to the divine perfection that can become the object of our deepest cravings. Against the background of Paul's theological reformulation of the concept of righteousness, Jesus' words in Beatitude Four can therefore be rendered in a more expansive form as follows: "Blessed are those who keep on hungering and thirsting after the righteousness of God which God himself makes accessible, for they will be satisfied."

We should also notice how this fourth Beatitude dynamizes the first one. The first Beatitude says that the pathway to God's kingdom can be found only by acknowledging one's bankrupt condition. By contrast, the fourth one says that having reached this stage, we should be committed to a continual hungering and thirsting after the righteousness that God himself provides.[3] This is the place where the quest begins and where we stand when we ask, "What should we do after we have made access to God's kingdom and after we have experienced the mourning and the meekness to which Jesus has already called our attention?" There is an element of passivity involved when one acknowledges his spiritual poverty and is willing to embrace the divine happiness that can be received simply as a gift. However, we want to know what occurs after we have received this gift; after we have faced tribulation; after we have reached down in gentleness; after we have inherited both heaven and the earth. In response, Jesus suggests that an outward journey which expresses itself in a continual hungering and thirsting for divine righteousness becomes appropriate at this point.

Notice how Jesus continues to develop this theme when he

claims in verse seven: "Blessed are the merciful, for they shall obtain mercy" (Mt 5.7). The righteous face is very rarely a merciful face![4] We see a righteous face from time to time, and it is very difficult for that face to be a face of mercy—*unless* the righteousness in question is the righteousness reflected in the face of Christ. But if this is the kind of righteousness for which we are hungering and thirsting, and if it is this kind of hungering and thirsting that Jesus proposes to satisfy, it then becomes possible for us to move on to verse seven where he says, "Blessed are the merciful." In this case, the righteousness of the righteous face is made possible through the mercy expressed already in the grace of God. If we transform the Beatitudes from merely ethical prescriptions into the richer versions Jesus intends to make visible, we will find a righteousness that makes mercy possible, for the righteousness in question comes through a gift given and received, and given away again.

It is very tempting to give people what they deserve. It is much harder to give them grace. Of course, several paradoxes lie hidden in this point. Often when we give people what they deserve we are saying more about ourselves than we are about them. For example, we sometimes give someone what he deserves with gritted teeth, and we thereby express in our actions so much about ourselves that lies twisted and hidden even from our own consciousness. But then there is the other side to be considered: mercy which gives us access to the grace of God is sometimes a gift that can be very tough and realistic. It can manifest itself not only in a gentle utterance, but also in a straightforward demand from us to another, or from another to us, calling us back to ourselves and forcing us to face the real order with responsible commitment. In giving people what they deserve, we often give them a slice of our hidden selves; while in giving them grace, we sometimes have to undertake the task of calling them back into the circle where God wants them to be. The teaching of the Sermon on the Mount is not to be reduced to the flimsy content from which the degenerate notion of the meek Christ has been fabricated.[5] It has the toughness of the carpenter's shop interlaced through it, and that dimension is woven in and through the grace of God freely given to us. "Blessed are the merciful who are merciful because they have found the only righteousness worth having, for they will receive mercy in return."

And this mercy will come first from God, then from us, and finally from somebody else.

Notice also verse eight where Jesus says, "Blessed are the pure in heart, for they shall see God" (Mt 5.8). Hungering and thirsting after righteousness, and the merciful life to which they lead, generate *a new nature* in the one in whom they occur. And Jesus describes this new nature in the phrase, "the pure in heart." On the surface this phrase might seem to have a merely ethical significance, but as in the earlier cases, nothing could be further from the truth. "Pure in heart" means "an undivided consciousness";[6] it means a consciousness no longer torn apart; it means a consciousness made whole. Thus Jesus tells us, "Blessed is the consciousness made whole because of righteousness on the one hand and mercy on the other, for a consciousness of this kind will attain a vision of God." This was the favorite Beatitude of the early Church Fathers, and this was so because they understood that only an undivided consciousness is able to catch a glimpse of God.

Before I attempt to bring the first six Beatitudes together, I should mention a crucial point that might be easily overlooked. You will notice that in each Beatitude the consequent is always expressed in the future tense. For example, "Blessed are the poor in spirit, for they *shall* inherit the kingdom of heaven," or "Blessed are the pure in heart, for they *shall* see God." The implication seems to be that what is in question is a state that will be realized in the future. However, the function of the future tense in the Greek text is to call our attention not to something that will happen later, but to an absolutely necessary consequence that will follow if the condition mentioned in the antecedent is fulfilled. "Blessed are the poor in spirit, for as a logical consequence, they will inherit the kingdom of heaven"; "Blessed are the pure in heart, for it follows necessarily that they will see God." The present tense of the fourth Beatitude carries us forward in a continual activity of hungering and thirsting, and the undivided consciousness to which it leads in Beatitude Six culminates in the vision of God, not simply in the future, but as a logical consequence of our undivided condition. In acknowledging our finitude, we are often far too reluctant to affirm the fact that God wishes to disclose himself to us. By contrast, Jesus says that the vision of God will follow necessarily from the undivided consciousness that the Beatitudes intend to produce.

In conclusion, let me illustrate the logical structure of the first six Beatitudes by introducing a picture that summarizes our earlier discussion. Let us draw a diamond with four sides and four angles that converge to four points,

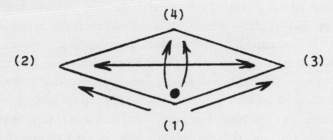

and let us reformulate the crucial points of our discussion with reference to this diagram. Blessed are those who are willing to acknowledge their poverty-stricken condition and who contract to a point (1), for when emptiness of this kind is acknowledged, we are given access to God's kingdom. And blessed are those who mourn, both for themselves and for the world (2 and 3), for as we move back and forth between the sinful self and the fragmented world, Jesus promises that we will be comforted. And blessed also are those who have unified these earlier stages in the gentle soul (4), for they shall not only inherit God's kingdom, but shall also inherit the earth.

Now let us return to the beginning and repeat the pattern, this time with respect to Beatitudes Four, Five, and Six:

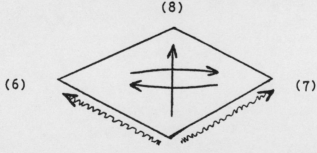

Having been poor in spirit (1), having mourned (2 and 3), and having embraced the gentle consciousness (4), we now return to the first stage of our journey, but this time dynamically. When this occurs, the point that has contracted into emptiness (1) begins to explode, hungering and thirsting for God's righteousness in a process that stretches out over a lifetime (5). And having done so, it stands at the second stage again, this time not only to mourn for itself and for the world, but also to show mercy, so that the relation between these two poles is not simply a transaction of discord (3 and 4), but is instead an expression of mercy that embraces a fragmented world (6 and 7). But then finally, blessed is the undivided consciousness, that has contracted to a point (1), that has mourned (2 and 3), that has become meek (4), that has hungered and thirsted continuously for righteousness (5), and that has shown mercy and received it from another (6 and 7), for that undivided consciousness shall also see God (8). So Jesus says: "Blessed is the empty self, for it shall inherit God's kingdom. Blessed are those that mourn, both for themselves and for the world, for they will be comforted. Blessed are the gentle, for they shall inherit the earth. Blessed are those who keep on hungering and thirsting for God's righteousness, for they shall be satisfied. Blessed are the merciful, for they shall obtain mercy. And finally, blessed is the fragmented consciousness made whole, for it shall be given a vision of God."

CHAPTER IV

PERSECUTION
AND THE REAL ORDER

❧

Before he turns to the last three Beatitudes Jesus says, "Blessed are the pure in heart, for they shall see God." And when we notice that the pure in heart is the undivided consciousness, we might very well think that he should have stopped there, for there is much to be said for the claim that the Beatitudes reach their highest expression in the vision of God. The sixth Beatitude takes us to the mountain top, and like Peter and John in another context, our response might be, "Lord, let us stay here, and let us build three tabernacles, moving from one to the next in a trinitarian celebration of absoluteness, unaffected by the discord of ordinary existence" (Mt 17.1–9). But what does Jesus say? Having spoken about the vision of God, he now suggests what he said to his disciples on that other occasion: "It is time to go back down the mountain and to hear the realistic message that is to be found in verse nine: 'Blessed are the peacemakers, for they shall be called the sons of God' " (Mt 5.9). Jesus will never allow us to see God's face without calling our attention back to the world. If there is a natural tendency to embrace the other-worldliness to which we are sometimes attracted, Jesus' words at this point are unequivocal: having seen God's face, we must turn back toward the real order and must embrace the task of reconciliation that will make it possible for us to be called God's children.

31

"Peacemaking" means "reconciliation," and peace always pre-supposes the reconciling act. However, the most important point to notice is that the first place where peace is required is in our relationship with God. Paul formulates the crucial point in theological terms in the second chapter of Ephesians:

> But now in Christ Jesus you who formerly were far off have been brought near by the blood of Christ. For He Himself is our peace, who made both groups into one, and broke down the barrier of the dividing wall, by abolishing in His flesh the enmity, which is the Law of commandments contained in ordinances, that in Himself He might make the two into one new man, thus establishing peace, and might reconcile them both in one body to God through the cross, by it having put to death the enmity. And He came and preached peace to you who were far away, and peace to those who were near; for through Him we both have our access in one Spirit to the Father (Eph 2.13–18).

Paul is of course referring to the two communities he confronts and to the two radically different worlds he is attempting to unite—one the Hebrew tradition from which he comes, and the other the Gentile community to which he is reaching out. But he insists that these two worlds can be reconciled only when the God of peace reconciles us to himself. Thus, within the human realm, a reference to peacemaking presupposes peace with God.

But peacemaking must not stop there, for it must have an outward thrust. The pure in heart must become purifying; those who have been reconciled must undertake the task of reconciliation; and those who have found peace with God must become the peacemakers to whom Jesus calls our attention in verse nine.[1] In developing this point in theological terms, Paul once more makes the issue explicit in the first chapter of II Corinthians:

> Therefore if any man is in Christ, he is a new creature; the old things are passed away; behold, new things have come. Now all these things are from God, who reconciled us to Himself through Christ, and gave us the ministry of reconciliation, namely that God was in Christ reconciling the world to Himself, not counting their trespasses against them, and He has committed to us the word of

reconciliation. Therefore, we are ambassadors for Christ, as though God were entreating through us; we beg you on behalf of Christ, be reconciled to God. He made Him who knew no sin to be sin on our behalf, that we might become the righteousness of God in Him (2 Cor 5.17–21).

What does peacemaking of the kind Jesus teaches and Paul attempts to explicate presuppose? It presupposes, in the first place, the empty self of the first Beatitude. Peacemaking presupposes that there are no hidden agendas, and the special poignancy of the act of peacemaking at its richest moments comes from the fact that the act is not performed merely to accomplish our own intentions. This kind of peacemaking is always appropriate, for its integrity is rooted in the empty self. One of the richest reflections of peacemaking in these terms is expressed in the journal of Dag Hammarskjöld, which he wrote when the curtains were drawn and the eighteen and nineteen hour days were over, amidst the discord and conflict of an active political existence. As one leafs through those pages, he finds that the writer had embraced the empty self and that without hidden intentions, he had taken up the task of reconciliation. For example, in 1954 Hammarskjöld wrote:

> Thou who art over us,
> Thou who are one of us,
> Thou who *art*—
> Also within us,
> May all see Thee—in me also,
> May I prepare the way for Thee,
> May I thank Thee for all that shall fall to my lot,
> May I also not forget the needs of others,
> Keep me in Thy love
> As Thou wouldest that all should be kept in mine.
> May everything in this my being be directed to Thy glory
> And may I never despair
> For I am under Thy hand,
> And in Thee is all power and goodness.
>
> Give me a pure heart—that I may see Thee,
> A humble heart—that I may hear Thee,
> A heart of love—that I may serve Thee,
> A heart of faith—that I may abide in Thee.[2]

In response, the reader can only say that whether the peacemaking act achieves its external purposes or not; whether it transforms the world or not; whether it brings unity or not within the social and political arenas in which it occurs—the crucial point is that the act itself be rooted in the empty self that has been reconciled with God, and whose acts of reconciliation will allow it to be called God's child.

However, it is important to notice that the peacemaking act not only presupposes the empty self, but that it also presupposes the undivided self. We sometimes attempt to make peace on the outside when what we are in fact attempting to find is peace within. And we sometimes embrace the problems of the larger world merely as a displacement for our own fragmented condition. I do not intend to suggest that peacemaking is always the expression of hidden intentions, nor am I implying that it always takes the form of attempting to do for another what we have been unable to do for ourselves. However, until peacemaking first reflects the empty self made whole, and until it reflects the focal unity that first becomes accessible in the vision of God, it will never succeed in expressing the unity it seeks. By contrast, it will always succeed at the most fundamental level if the act of bringing peace is grounded in those other places. Thus, it is not by accident that verse nine tells us, "Blessed are the peacemakers, for they will be the sons of God." Jesus wants his followers to become replicas of God, and as a result, he suggests that peacemaking presupposes God's primary act of reconciliation in which we already participate. In fact, the act of bringing peace to another acquires its significance from the fact that it is God's offspring and that it brings the reconciling act of God himself to bear upon the human realm.

In Beatitude Seven, Jesus turns away from the mountain top toward the larger world, inviting us to embrace the task of reconciliation in the light of the reconciliation we have already experienced. However, in Beatitude Eight he suggests that when we do so, we must be prepared to confront radical opposition. Thus verse ten tells us: "Blessed are those who have been persecuted for the sake of righteousness, for theirs is the kingdom of heaven" (Mt 5.10). No doubt Jesus already anticipates the storm clouds that will gather in his own life, and indeed, in the experience of those who are listening to him. And in direct response to this anticipated disruption he suggests that peace-making brings persecution, and that it does so as a natural conse-quence. Of course, Jesus wishes that persecution could be avoided, for as he himself would pray in the garden: "Father, take this cup away from me" (Mt 26.39). However, the most important fact about this episode is that he would also pray, "Nevertheless, not my will, but your will be done." In that moment peacemaking and persecution come together, and we are given access once more to the kingdom of God.

Why does Jesus say at the end of verse ten something he has said already at the end of verse three? Why does he say "Blessed are those who have been persecuted, for theirs is the kingdom of heaven," when this same kingdom has already been made accessible to the poor in spirit? In the first case, entrance into God's kingdom becomes possible because one admits his absolute bankruptcy and in that moment becomes a citizen of a new realm. But having made access to a kingdom that lies beyond, Jesus also suggests that when we are persecuted for righteousness sake, and when because of peacemaking persecution comes, we will inherit this same kingdom within the concrete context of our daily existence. The kingdom is both beyond and here, and we gain entrance into what lies beyond by confessing our poverty-stricken condition. But how does the kingdom not sim-ply remain beyond, but also become the kingdom coming, and the kingdom come? It becomes so when peacemaking, having endured persecution, leads us into a new order that can be present here and now. We make initial access to God's kingdom by admitting that we are empty and bankrupt. But when through peacemaking and per-secution we embody the reconciling act of God in acts of our own, the kingdom that lies beyond becomes accessible within the human realm.

These reflections finally bring us to verses eleven and twelve, where Jesus says: "Blessed are you when men revile you and persecute you, and say all kinds of evil against you falsely on account of Me. Rejoice and be glad, for your reward in heaven is great, for so they persecuted the prophets who were before you" (Mt 5.11,12). In what respect does this ninth Beatitude develop the content of what has just been said? Persecution is at the center again, and as a result, these verses might appear to be repetitious. But there is another dimension of Beatitude Nine that is not present before, and that additional element is joy. Of course, divine happiness has bracketed our entire discussion. Happiness of this kind is a crucial part of what the word "blessed" means, and this word is the foundation upon which the nine Beatitudes stand. However, in the ninth Beatitude, Jesus takes the blessedness that brackets everything he says and moves it into the center of his teaching, saying at this point, "Blessed are those who are insulted, who are persecuted, and who are slandered because of me. Rejoice and be glad, for great is your reward in heaven." In this way, peacemaking which has confronted persecution finally erupts into the positive and focused fullness of divine blessedness, and joy comes to stand at the center of our fragmented existence.

But why does Jesus add the phrase, "for my sake"? Apparently, it is not so crucial that we be insulted, or so important that we be persecuted and slandered, but that we be prepared to endure both for his sake. The grace of God is the place and Jesus is the focal point where the world has been inverted and where he has asked us to stand, and the suggestion of his entire message is that only if we stand there do these nine Beatitudes mean anything. What Jesus is discussing here is the resentment that arises in the larger world when it is confronted by the inversion that takes place in the confession of spiritual bankruptcy, and when it is asked to embrace the kind of reconciliation that can only spring from the empty self. When a reconciling act of this kind occurs and when it encounters insults on the one hand and slander on the other, Jesus says that at that moment, our joy becomes full. "Blessed are you when men revile you, and persecute you, and say all kinds of evil against you falsely *for my sake*. Rejoice and be glad, for great is your reward in heaven."

What shall we say in conclusion about the last phrase in verse twelve, "for great is your reward in heaven"? At this point Jesus is not speaking simply about entering God's kingdom, but about the rewards to be found there. He is also pointing by implication to the Last Judgment, a detailed description of which is to be found in verses twelve through fifteen of the twentieth chapter of Revelation:

And I saw the dead, the great and the small, standing before the throne, and books were opened: and another book was opened, which is the book of life; and the dead were judged from the things which were written in the books, according to their deeds. And the sea gave up the dead which were in it, and death and Hades gave up the dead which were in them; and they were judged, every one of them according to their deeds. And death and Hades were thrown into the lake of fire. This is the second death, the lake of fire. And if anyone's name was not found written in the book of life, he was thrown into the lake of fire (Rv 20.12–15).

What is John suggesting here as a way of understanding the rewards to which Jesus refers? When we stand at the Last Judgment, there are a number of dimensions of the situation that might well be unexpected. For example, sin will not be there. The sins in which you and I are entangled have been paid for, and God has promised that he has blotted them out and that he will "remember them against us no more" (Heb 8.12). Thus, the question to be confronted at the Last Judgment is not the problem of sin, for Jesus has dealt with it already. However, there is a second factor about the judgment that must be taken into account, and which in John's words are called "deeds." Would we be shocked to learn that those deeds are good deeds? Or would be surprised to discover that they are the deeds that countless generations have performed in order to merit the grace of God that can simply be received as a gift? If we read between the lines, John seems to be suggesting that when the books which record our deeds are opened, the ones standing there will not be judged because of their sins, but because of their deeds, the doing of which has come to function as the surrogate for saying, "Lord, be merciful to me a sinner." At the throne of judgment, self-righteousness stands opposed to the righteousness of God, and it will be judged defective as a condition for receiving the rewards he wishes to bestow upon his followers.

Yet there is a third factor that must also be considered when we focus on the Last Judgment. Sins will not be there; good deeds will be there in abundance; but John also tells us that the Book of Life will be there as well. And notice that no one will receive a reward because of the deeds written in those other books unless his name is also written in the Book of Life. But what happens if one's name is written there? Whatever good deeds are also there can then be what they are because of the grace that has come from God, and those deeds will not be good in themselves, but good because they are an expression of God's reconciling acts of grace toward the world. There are two ways to read the Beatitudes. One is as a set of ethical prescriptions which have a merely humanistic and edifying significance: "Blessed are the poor in spirit"; "Blessed are they that mourn"; "Blessed are the meek"; "Blessed are those who hunger and thirst after righteousness"; "Blessed are the merciful"; "Blessed are the pure in heart"; "Blessed are the peacemakers"; "Blessed are the persecuted"; and "Blessed are those who must face insults and slander as they confront the real order." In these terms, the sayings of Jesus merely become the charter for an elevated ethical existence and will never produce the rewards to which he wishes to call our attention.

But what happens when behind the Beatitudes we see the grace of God and confront the face of Christ in whom he has chosen to express himself? Then we can say, "Blessed are those who are bankrupt and who acknowledge what God has done for us, for theirs is the kingdom of heaven"; "Blessed are those who mourn under the extreme pressure of daily existence, for they will be comforted by God's spirit"; "Blessed are the gentle, who have reached that stage because God has first reached them, for they will inherit the earth"; "Blessed are those who hunger and thirst after God's righteousness, for they will be satisfied"; "Blessed are the merciful who are merciful because God has first been merciful to them, for they shall obtain mercy from others"; "Blessed is the unified consciousness made whole by the work of Christ, for it will see God"; "Blessed are the peacemakers who are reconciling the world because God has already reconciled them, for they shall be called the children of God"; "Blessed are those who are persecuted daily as his followers, for theirs is the kingdom of heaven"; and finally, "Blessed are those who are ridiculed, and slandered, and insulted for his sake, for great is their reward in heaven." And in this case, the reward is great because the deeds of his followers are finite expressions of God's work in the world through them.

CHAPTER V

TWO OVERARCHING METAPHORS:
THE SALT OF THE EARTH
AND THE LIGHT OF THE WORLD

❧

In our study of the Beatitudes we have found that the initial teaching of Jesus expresses a fourfold focus. In the first place, it points to divine inner happiness that can obtain *no matter what the external circumstances may be*. Every time Jesus says "blessed," he means to imply that divine happiness is accessible, that it can exist inside the soul, and that it can exist there in the midst of the extreme pressure that is often encountered in the course of daily existence. Thus Jesus suggests that the happiness to which he calls his followers is a gift that can transcend the fragmentation into which the finite consciousness so easily falls.

In the second place, the blessings referred to in the Beatitudes are *meaningless apart from a relationship with God*. It is possible to read the Beatitudes as though they were ethical teachings that can be detached from the larger context in which they are rooted, but in the end, it is impossible to understand their significance unless we see that God himself stands behind them. We have found that the Beatitudes can be organized into three groups of three, and as a result, we have discussed their internal structure in triadic terms. However, the crucial point to notice is that there is a fourth term that makes all the difference, and that this fourth term which undergirds the claims of Jesus is *God himself.* Jesus suggests that apart from a relationship with God it is unintelligible to speak about poverty of spirit; apart from this relationship it is impossible to talk about the absolute satisfaction that comes to our deepest longings; and apart from it, mercy is impossible, the vision of God is impossible, and it is also impossible to receive rewards within God's kingdom. So however the structure of our discussion might proceed internally, sustaining it is always a response to God elicited by the content of the message itself.

In the third place, we find that throughout the Beatitudes *Jesus moves back and forth between an inner and an outer dimension.* For example, he speaks about those who are prepared to declare their spiritual bankruptcy, and therefore points to the inner dimension that must be at the center of the new life he comes to bring. But having said that we must be poor in spirit to enter God's kingdom, he adds, "Blessed are those who mourn, not only for their own condition but also for the larger world, for they will be comforted." And as the subsequent discussion unfolds, we find Jesus moving from the inner to the outer dimensions and back again, trying to bring the core of our existence into relation with the larger world in which we are asked to live. In doing so, he suggests that the divine inner happiness which obtains regardless of circumstances, and which depends upon a positive relationship with God, begins on the inside, but has relevance to the larger world as well.

Finally, in verses ten through twelve Jesus suggests that some of the blessings he gives us *will be given in this world, and that they will often be given amidst extreme persecution.* What begins as an invitation into God's heavenly kingdom ends with a reference to persecution; what begins as an internal condition ends as an encounter with radical opposition; and what begins as a divine blessing becomes in the end a message that has a positive bearing on the real order in which we are placed. Jesus says that divine happiness not only comes to those who stand in a positive relationship with him, but also to those who having gone inside to find their emptiness, reach outside to put themselves in touch with a larger world, finding there the utterly realistic fact of discord and persecution. In these nine verses, Jesus reaches his arms around the cosmos—from the heights to the depths, from what is inside to what lies beyond—and in doing so, he binds all these dimensions together with a promise of divine happiness that God himself makes accessible.

As we continue our discussion by turning to verses thirteen through sixteen of Chapter Five, we find that the outward thrust of the Beatitudes is accentuated. In fact, I believe these verses can be understood best as a commentary on what has just gone before, and as an attempt to emphasize the relevance of Jesus' teaching to the real order. This outward dimension of the message is expressed in verse thirteen where Jesus says:

> You are the salt of the earth; but if the salt has become tasteless, how will it be made salty again? It is good for nothing anymore, except to be thrown out and trampled under foot by men (Mt 5.13).

Notice that Jesus is addressing young fishermen who have turned away from their initial occupation to follow him and that this is one of the first opportunities he has had to teach them. What does he say to these men, concerned about their own situation in a politically chaotic context, and having a variety of alternatives before them about the kind of life they ought to embrace within this context? He says triumphantly, "You are the salt of the earth," thus addressing them from the outset in cosmic terms.[1]

It has often been suggested that salt has three characteristics that are clearly relevant to Jesus' intentions. In the first place, salt is different from the medium in which it is placed, for unless it differs from its context, it can never do its work. So in the first place Jesus says, "You are the salt of the earth in contrast with the earth itself." In the second place, salt has a preservative function, and therefore, the salt that differs from its medium is also intended to preserve it. In this way, the initial moment of difference is transformed into a positive task. Finally, Jesus makes it clear that salt not only preserves but also flavors, and that it is the task of the disciples to embrace this positive role.[2] The salt of the earth to which Jesus refers has a threefold function, sustaining the difference between itself and its medium while it preserves and flavors as well.

It is especially important to notice that the purpose of this verse is not to express a compliment, but to formulate a warning. To say in ordinary English that someone is the salt of the earth is usually to express a positive appraisal, however qualified this appraisal might be. But remember that Jesus not only says, "You are the salt of the earth," but adds, "if the salt becomes tasteless, how will it be made salty again? It is good for nothing anymore, except to be thrown out and trampled under the feet of men." What appears to be a compliment in the first clause becomes a warning in the second, and as a result, the focus of our attention shifts from the positive dimension of the first phrase to the negative element implicit in the second.

The voice, the tense, and the mood of the verb in the phrase before us are absolutely crucial. "Has become tasteless" is a passive verb, which suggests that the state Jesus mentions can simply happen to us. Moreover, this same verb is in the aorist tense, which implies that the state in question can begin at a particular moment in time. Finally, the mood of the verb is subjunctive, which suggests that whether or not this condition occurs depends on us. The passive verb implies that this condition can steal over us if we take our eyes off the one speaking to us here. The aorist tense suggests that this can occur at a particular moment, and that when it does, one can become insipid very quickly. But the subjunctive mood also reminds us that whether this occurs or not depends upon us, and that as a result, we have a choice to make in the matter. Having formulated a series of blessings that culminate in a vision of rewards in heaven, Jesus returns very quickly to the earth to frame a description of a difficult task and to formulate a warning for his followers: "You are the salt of the earth, but if you become useless as salt, you are good for nothing but to be trampled under the feet of men." And of course, the result in this case is that trampling will replace persecution and that it will do so because we are no longer worth anything. When the follower of Christ loses his savoring quality, the result is utter tastelessness, and when this occurs, we are no longer persecuted and insulted, but are merely cast out to the side of the road.

The purpose of this verse is not to focus our attention on the concept of salvation, but upon the task to which the Christian has been called within the larger world. As the gospel emphasizes again and again, when we have responded to the grace of God and have been made whole, we need not fear that we can ever be lost again. However, it is indeed possible for us to turn away from our task, and when this occurs again and again, the result will sometimes be the sheer tastelessness from which we can never recover our original vibrancy. When the world casts us aside because of our insipidity, it is not able to take us out of our Father's hand. Nevertheless, the reaction of the world to the gospel might well be to turn away in disgust unless we heed the warning expressed so clearly in this passage. Having entered God's kingdom, we are asked to become the salt of the earth. If we cease to perform this vital task and persistently turn away from it, we will not only be cast aside, but will perhaps never be able to recover the original function we have been called to embrace.

Notice that having pointed to this crucial function by saying, "You are the salt of the earth," Jesus now shifts the metaphor in verse fourteen and says, "You are the light of the world. A city set on a hill cannot be hidden" (Mt 5.14). What is the difference between salt and light? As Stanley Jones suggests, salt works *silently,* it works *pervasively,* it works *unobtrusively*; by contrast, the light is *open and manifest.*[3] So Jesus says first that we are the salt of the earth—silently, pervasively, unobtrusively; and having said that, he says next that we are the light of the world—open and manifest. Perhaps we should emphasize the fact that the order of these metaphors reflects the inward and the outward dimensions of Jesus' earlier teaching, expressed on this occasion in relation to the larger world. We must be transformed within before we can display an outward manifestation; we must become salt before we can become light; and salt must do its silent work before it can burst forth into flame. Without mixing the metaphors, we shift from the one to the next so that the one who has become the salt of the earth can become the light of the world. We sometimes wish for light, and we sometimes wish to be light without having heeded the requirement for the saltiness of the first part of the message. Salt first, then light; silence first, then visible manifestation; unobtrusiveness first, and then the manifest openness of the light of the world.

It is crucial to remember that Jesus says in this verse, "*You* are the light of the world," because this reference reminds us of another context in which he says something remarkably similar about himself. Every year the Feast of Lights is celebrated in the Hebrew tradition, and when it was celebrated in the time of Jesus, the practice was for lamps to be placed inside the Temple in Jerusalem on each one of eight days—Sabbath through Sabbath. For eight days the priests lit the lamps in the Temple, and from the hill in Jerusalem where the Temple stood, those lights could be seen beyond the city. Unfortunately, after the second Sabbath *the lights went out,* and the people were required to wait another year for them to be relit. Thus, it was not by accident that Jesus appeared in the Temple on Sunday morning when the Feast of Lights was over to say to his disciples, "I am the light of the world" (Jn 8.12). That is to say, "When the lights that can be seen around the city have gone out, I have come to light up the world in a fashion that can never be extinguished."

Prepared as he was to say this about himself, notice what he says to his disciples in this passage in the present tense: "You *keep on being* the light of the world." As I have suggested already, the present tense in Greek points to continuous action, not calling our attention to a momentary occurrence, but to a stretched-out action. By implication, Jesus says, "I came into the world to bring light; I have planted that light within you; now, you keep on being the light of the world so that when the lights go out in the Temple when the Feast of Lights is over, they can be replaced by the light that comes from God and than can be re-expressed on countless occasions by the light shining in your own lives." Notice also that it is no accident that Jesus refers in this passage to a "city set on a hill." He no doubt has Jerusalem in mind; perhaps he has a mental picture of how that hill was lighted up when the Temple lights were shining; but he also has in mind the hillside where he is now addressing his disciples. Where are those who are to keep on being the light of the world? They are the ones seated beside him who are responding to his teaching.

Let us now consider verse fifteen where Jesus says: "Nor do men light a lamp, and put it under the peck-measure, but on the lamp-stand; and it gives light to all who are in the house" (Mt 5.15). The reference to a peck-measure is important, for the peck-measure was the standard in terms of which farmers at the time of Jesus transacted their affairs.[4] Thus, the injunction against placing one's light under what we usually call "the bushel" is a warning not to allow the usual measure by which we transact business to be the standard *so that the light goes out*. All of us are faced with the question: "Where is the light from beyond, the light come down, the light within, and the light of the world to be placed?" If we answer by placing that light under the peck-measure by which we conduct our ordinary affairs, it will be stifled and will cease to play its illuminating role within the larger world.

But what can we do instead? We can place the light on top of the basket with which we sort and measure our ordinary affairs so that this time the peck-measure is inverted, letting it become the lamp-stand where the light of the world shines. When the peck-measure is in place, it becomes the standard by which we sort our way through the world, and when it functions in this way, it is turned upward as an instrument with which we do our work. But notice what Jesus says: "Do not put the light of the world *under* that basket; do not put that light under the standard by which you measure your ordinary affairs; but instead, embrace the alternative to which you have been called as my disciples." We must keep on measuring and sorting, for we can never escape the finite context in which we are embedded. However, it is also possible to embrace our finite task with the basket *inverted,* and with the light placed on top so that it becomes a lamp-stand for the world. Jesus says, "Do not place your light under a peck-measure, but on a lampstand, so that it can give light to all those who are in the house."

Notice finally verse sixteen: "Let your light shine before men in such a way that they may see your good works, and glorify your Father who is in heaven" (Mt 5.16). The shining of the light to which Jesus refers in this passage is expressed in the imperative mood. Moreover, the tense of the verb implies that the light in question must shine in the lives of his followers as a series of reflections of his light in the world. But remember that there is also a relationship between the light mentioned here and what Jesus calls our "good works." He has just demanded that we become the light of the world, but now he adds, "let your light so shine that others may see your way of acting, and glorify your Father who is in heaven."

In considering this passage, it is important to emphasize the fact that our good deeds are not identical with the light, but are the actions that result from our willingness to let the light shine. The light in question has come down from above; it has shined in the world; Jesus has asked us to let it shine back; but now, when that light is placed on top of the peck-measure, its effect is to light up what we do so that others can see. The light itself is not the works, but is rather the source of illumination that allows those works to become visible. Therefore, we must distinguish between the light that shines within and the good works that are made visible thereby. Notice once more how the crucial passage reads: "Let your light shine before men in such a way that they may see your good works." The good works we produce are illuminated by the light that shines, but this shining light is not to be identified with the works themselves.

The light within results from our having admitted our bankrupt condition and having been admitted into God's kingdom. When this occurs, the light from beyond becomes the light within and is the principle that allows us to reflect the light that comes from God. But now Jesus suggests, "Let the light within light up what you do so that those who see it can appraise your works as good, and they will see them as good in the appropriate sense only if what is done is lighted up by the light that comes from above." Jesus has asked us to let our light shine, not putting it under the peck-measure of our everyday affairs. Now he adds a further consideration: when the light is placed on the lampstand of our daily existence, our works within that ordinary context can be appraised as "good" only in the light that comes from God.

Jesus makes this point explicit in the final phrase of verse sixteen, where he tells us that the purpose of our good deeds is to permit others to "glorify our Father in heaven." What does the word "glorify" mean in this context? It means simply "to acknowledge God's perfection." Returning once more to our original metaphor, we find that the light was first with God; that it then came down;

that Jesus said, "I am the light of the world"; that he tells us to keep on being the light of the world; and that he asks us to do this by turning the bushel basket of our daily existence upside down so that the light within can shine on the lampstand of our ordinary affairs. Then in verse sixteen he says, "Let your light so shine that others will be able to see your way of acting in this ordinary context and appraise it as 'good,' *which will in turn allow them to acknowledge the perfection of God.*" In this way, their attention can be drawn to the light that has come down from above, to the light that lights up the world, to the light within, to the light shining on the lampstands that we display to the world, and finally *to the divine goodness of which our own good deeds are simply a finite expression.*

PART II

THE PAST AND THE FUTURE: FIVE PRACTICAL PROBLEMS

CHAPTER VI

JESUS AS THE FULFILLMENT
OF TRADITION

In the first sixteen verses of the Sermon on the Mount, Jesus calls his disciples to embrace a new way of life, and in the process he bestows nine blessings upon them which display both inward and outward dimensions. For example, Jesus addresses those who are poor in spirit, those that mourn, those who are gentle, and those who are pure in heart, and he says that divine happiness will be given to his followers if their lives display these four inner conditions. Jesus also tells us that divine happiness will be made accessible to those who hunger and thirst for righteousness, to those who show the same mercy to the larger world that they have received from him, to those who bring the same kind of peace to others that has been wrought within their own souls, and to those who encounter persecution within this larger context as they confront the extreme pressure of daily existence. Therefore, the Beatitudes that Jesus bestows upon his followers speak not only about divine blessings, but also about the inner and the outer dimensions of the human soul to which these blessings are addressed.

Jesus elaborates the outward thrust of his message in the concrete illustrations he gives in verses thirteen through sixteen. In this passage he says, "You are the salt of the earth, and you are the light of the world," thus hurling the Beatitudes out toward the rim of the world in metaphors that exhibit cosmic proportions. However, it is also important to notice that the specific character of the metaphors Jesus chooses reasserts the inward and the outward dimensions of his earlier teaching. Salt works quietly, it works silently, it works unobtrusively; and only after it has done its silent work does the light begin to shine as both open and manifest. The inward working to which one dimension of the Beatitudes has pointed thus becomes the outward manifestation of what Jesus describes as the light of the world. Salt works best when it loses itself; and in losing itself, the poverty of spirit to which Jesus refers in the first Beatitude is reinstated in the language he uses to develop his earlier thought. Salt also does its best work in an elevated temperature, and therefore, it is most effective when it is near the light within—shining, illuminating, and making visible the work of salt in the world. Yet in elaborating the role of his followers as the light of the world, Jesus also suggests that the purpose of their work should be to call the attention of the larger world to the Light that shines from beyond. The light within is derivative upon the Light that Jesus displays; the light that he wants his disciples to become presupposes the Light that has already come; and the light that shines from within is able to do its work because the Light of the world has already expressed itself in the words addressed to us here.

But how does Jesus begin to develop his thought after the new world to which the Beatitudes point has been announced and after he has begun to draw their cosmic implications in the metaphors he introduces? In the remainder of Chapter Five, he does this by turning to a detailed discussion of the relationship between his new teaching and the context out of which it emerges. Jesus knows that what he has said already might very well be regarded as a radical departure from the Hebrew tradition, and for this reason, he attempts to connect his teaching with the expectations and the past experiences of his audience. Most new ideas are oriented almost exclusively toward the future, looking backward to their origins only occasionally. Knowing this, and knowing that his followers will wonder about the relation between his new teaching and the old world with which they are familiar, Jesus responds in verse seventeen with a striking affirmation of the traditional teaching: "Do not think that I came to abolish the Law and the Prophets; I did not come to abolish, but to fulfill" (Mt 5.17).

This unequivocal affirmation of the past is surprising, for as the audience Jesus addressed listened to his message, the foundations of the Hebrew tradition began to shake beneath their feet. Jesus did not speak primarily about worship in the Temple but about the Law written on the heart; and in his daily activities, he often seemed to call into question the entire tradition from which his teaching originated. In the Gospel of Mark, there are several illustrations of the way in which Jesus seems to do this, both with respect to what he says and with respect to what he does. One example of this tendency is to be found in the second chapter of Mark as it pertains to the custom of fasting:

> And John's disciples and the Pharisees were fasting; and they came and said to Him, "Why do John's disciples and the disciples of the Pharisees fast, but your disciples do not fast?" And Jesus said to them, "While the bridegroom is with them, the attendants of the bridegroom do not fast, do they? So long as they have the bridegroom with them, they cannot fast" (Mk 2.18,19).

A similar rejection of tradition is expressed again at the conclusion of this same chapter, this time with respect to behavior that is appropriate on the Sabbath day:

> And it came about that He was passing through the grainfields on the Sabbath, and His disciples began to make their way along while picking the heads of grain. And the Pharisees were saying to Him, "See here, why are they doing what is not lawful on the Sabbath?" And He said to them, "Have you never read what David did when he was in need and became hungry, he and his companions: how he entered into the house of God in the time of Abiathar the high priest, and ate the consecrated bread, which is not lawful for anyone to eat except the priests, and he gave it also to those who were with him?" And He [kept] saying to them, *"The Sabbath was made for man, and not man for the Sabbath. Consequently, the Son of Man is Lord even of the Sabbath"* (Mk 2.23–28).

The imperfect tense of the first verb in this passage suggests that as Jesus and his disciples were walking through the grainfields, the Pharisees asked repeatedly, "Why are you doing what is unlawful on the Sabbath?" But having mentioned the earlier episode from the life of David in a single sentence, the imperfect tense of the third verb in this same passage also implies that Jesus responded to the grumblings of the Pharisees by saying again and again, "The Sabbath was made for man and not man for the Sabbath. Consequently, the Son of man is Lord even of the Sabbath."

Finally, the seventh chapter of Mark records another episode in which the practice of Jesus and his disciples appears to collide with the traditional Jewish teaching about purification:

> And the Pharisees and some of the scribes gathered together around Him when they had come from Jerusalem, and had seen that some of His disciples were eating their bread with impure hands, that is, unwashed. (For the Pharisees and all the Jews do not eat unless they carefully wash their hands, thus observing the traditions of the elders. . . .) And the Pharisees and the scribes asked Him, "Why do Your disciples not walk according to the tradition of the elders, but eat their bread with impure hands?" And He said to them, "Rightly did Isaiah prophesy of you hypo-crites, as it [stands] written, 'This people honors Me with their lips, but their heart is far away from Me. But in vain do they worship Me, teaching as doctrines the precepts of men.' Neglect-ing the commandment of God, you hold to the tradition of men" (Mk 7.1–8).

In the light of examples of this kind, it is not surprising that the disciples expected Jesus to say that he had come to destroy the past. However, in response to this expectation, he says in verse seventeen: "Do not assume that I have come to abolish the Law or the Prophets; I did not come to abolish, but to fulfill."

In attempting to understand Jesus' positive reference to the past, it is first necessary to distinguish between two kinds of law. There is on the one hand the threefold law of the Old Testament tradition that can be clearly articulated: first the moral law, expressed most clearly in the Ten Commandments; in the second place, the spiritual law, in which some of the prescriptions about Temple worship are clearly reflected in the sacrificial act that Jesus would one day perform; and in the third place, the social code, designed to make it possible for the nation of Israel to make the transition from slavery to freedom and to enable Moses to forge a collection of former slaves into a genuine community. By contrast, there is a second kind of law which scholars built around this original tradition, and which consisted in a set of commentaries written about it. It is this context Jesus has in mind when he says: "You are neglecting the commandment of God and obeying the traditions of men." On the one hand, we have the Law itself, shining forth in all its brilliance; on the other hand, we have the commentaries of men, which are much more problematic. Jesus wants his followers to grasp this distinction, for it is finally this contrast that will enable them to understand his remarks about the destruction and the fulfillment of the Law.

Even with respect to the Law in the best sense, it must be acknowledged that the concept of fulfillment points in two directions. When Jesus says that he has not come to destroy but to fulfill the Law, the notion of fulfillment involves putting an end to something in one sense so that it can flower forth in another.[1] Every fulfillment is both a death and a resurrection, and we can point to both dimensions by suggesting that it is first necessary for the Law to pass away before it can be fulfilled. But what was the purpose of the Law in the first instance? What was its basic intention? Why was it established as such a fundamental element of the Hebrew tradition? The primary purpose of the Law was not to regulate an unruly and unmanageable nation, but to make fellowship with God possible. As a result, the Law itself is not fundamental, but derivative upon the task of bringing the people to whom it is addressed into a harmonious relationship with God. It is thus not surprising that Jesus summarizes the entire content of the Law in such simple and straightforward terms in the twenty-second chapter of Matthew:

> "You shall love the Lord your God with all your heart, and with all your soul, and with all your mind." This is the great and foremost commandment. The second is like it, "You shall love your neighbor as yourself." On these two commandments depend the Law and the Prophets (Mt 22.37–40).

When Jesus says that he has not come to destroy the Law and the Prophets but to bring them to fulfillment, he no doubt has the Law and the Prophets in this fundamental sense in mind.

There is another consideration which must be taken into account, for it poses a genuine problem. If the intention of the Law is to make fellowship with God possible, why does it fail? Why is the history of the Hebrew tradition a history of failure to obey the Law, and why do the Prophets point so consistently to this abysmal failure of their own people? The only scriptural answer to this question is that the Law fails because of sin and that the fundamental intention of the Prophets is to call the Hebrew people back to fellowship with God. But how should we respond to the failure of the Law as it is expressed by the prophetic tradition and as it stands in contrast with the fragmented condition of those it addresses? There are only two responses which Jesus ever considers seriously, the first of which is pharisaical. When scholars confronted the Law, they wrote commentaries about it, seeking to spell out precisely what would be required to obey the Law in the face of sin, both intellectual, moral, and emotional. The presumption was that if the commentaries could be rich enough to spell out every implication of the original text, then to obey the commentaries would be to measure up to the Law's requirements. However, the tragedy of such an approach is twofold. In the first place, something essential will always be neglected in any commentary, no matter how comprehensive it may be. In the second place, scholarly preoccupation with exhaustive commentaries often serves to divert the attention of those who attend to them away from the original text to the commentaries themselves. It is just such a predicament to which Jesus points when he accuses the Pharisees of neglecting the commandments of God by focusing on the traditions of men.

What is the alternative response to the problem of sin and the Law which Jesus himself embraces? In claiming that he has not come to abolish but to fulfill the Law, he suggests that he will one day deal with the problem of the failure of the Law in his own life and work. The primary purpose of the Law was to make fellowship with God possible; the predicament that prevents fellowship of this kind is sin; the only way to fulfill the Law is for sin itself to be dealt with; and Jesus himself intends to deal with it by bringing the Law to completion. That is why the Gospel of John is able to say not that Jesus wrote anything, not primarily that he spoke anything, but rather, and most fundamentally, that *he was something*. The Living Word made flesh dealt with the problem of sin on the cross, and that one act makes all the commentaries upon the Law pale into insignificance in comparison with it.

Let me point briefly to a passage in the Book of Romans which can help us understand in theological terms what Jesus means when he claims that he has come, not to abolish the Law, but to fulfill it. Notice that these words come from a "Hebrew of the Hebrews" and from one who sat at Gamaliel's feet in Jerusalem as a student of the most well-known rabbi of the day (Phil 3.5). Nevertheless, Paul says:

> There is therefore now no condemnation for those who are in Christ Jesus. For the law of the Spirit of life in Christ Jesus has set you free from the law of sin and death. For what the Law could not do, weak as it was through the flesh, God did: sending His own Son in the likeness of sinful flesh and as an offering for sin, He condemned sin in the flesh, *in order that the requirement of the Law might be fulfilled in us,* who do not walk according to the flesh, but according to the Spirit (Rom 8.1–4).

Biblical interpreters who are fond of drawing a radical distinction between the simple teachings of Jesus and the complex theological speculations of Paul should focus on this passage as it pertains to Jesus' claim to bring the Law to completion. Paul tells us that Jesus did what the Law, because of its weakness through the flesh, could not do in order that the requirement of the Law might be *fulfilled* in us. The origins of the Hebrew tradition are to be found in the Law and in the relationship with God that the Law makes possible. In attempting to preserve and to bring these origins to fulfillment, we have then a statement of Jesus to his closest followers which can be reformulated in theological terms as follows: "I want to make fellowship with God possible, for that is what the Law intended. It failed because of your sin. It is my task to bring a remedy, and the way to do this is to bring the Law and the Prophets to completion in my own life and work."

But notice how Jesus develops this point in verse eighteen: "For truly I say to you, until heaven and earth pass away, not the smallest letter or stroke shall pass away from the Law, until all is fulfilled" (Mt 5.18). Jesus begins this verse with the words, "Truly I say to you." In the original text the word for truth refers to what is genuine as opposed to counterfeit or worthless currency, calling our attention to the positive value of what he is about to say. But having begun in this way, he quickly adds, "until heaven and earth pass away in their present form, not the smallest letter or stroke shall pass away from the Law until all is accomplished." The phrase, "the smallest letter or stroke," refers to the smallest letter of the Hebrew alphabet, and to one of the strokes that might appear over the letter in question. Thus Jesus tells us that the most minute detail of the Law will not vanish until everything is accomplished. However, this final formulation shifts our attention once more to the notion of accomplishment and raises the question explicitly, "What is it to accomplish the Law?" In the Gospel of John, Jesus says that his task is "to complete the work of Him who sent me" (Jn 4.34). On the cross, he asks for a drink so that he can cry out to all who can hear him, "It stands finished" (Jn 19.30). And in the second chapter of Philippians, Paul concludes the great *knosis* passage by pointing to the concept of fulfillment in the following words:

> Therefore also God highly exalted Him, and bestowed [upon] Him the name which is above every name, that at the name of Jesus every knee should bow, of those who are in heaven, and on earth, and under the earth, and that every tongue should confess that Jesus Christ is Lord, to the glory of God the Father (Phil 2.9–11).

There is a threefold way that the Lord of the Sabbath brings the Law and the Prophets to fulfillment: he does so on the cross; he does so in his resurrection; and he does so in his final exaltation. The intention of this verse can thus be expressed in theological terms by saying: *the Law stands until everything is accomplished*—cross, resurrection, and exaltation. Now of course, Jesus is just beginning to teach his disciples, long before the cross, the resurrection, and the ascension, but even at this juncture he suggests that not one letter or stroke would vanish from the law until all these things are accomplished.

There are a number of problems that this interpretation of the concept of fulfillment introduces, but the commentary that puts us at the center of these problems begins in verse nineteen of this same chapter. Having said that the Law will not pass away until everything is accomplished, Jesus adds:

> Whoever then annuls one of the least of these commandments, and so teaches others, shall be called least in the kingdom of heaven; but whoever keeps and teaches them, he shall be called great in the kingdom of heaven (Mt 5.19).

In order to face the implications of this passage, we must first attempt to answer a number of questions. How can we stand under grace and not under the Law, if the Law cannot be annulled until everything is accomplished? What is the role of the Law within the context of the grace of God? And if the one who makes divine happiness accessible fulfills the Law by an act that we cannot perform for ourselves, why are we still bound to the requirements of the Law as this verse clearly seems to imply?

In responding to these questions, we must first remember that the purpose of the Law was to make fellowship with God possible. As Jesus says in the twenty-second chapter of Matthew: "You shall love the Lord your God with all your heart, and with all your soul, and with all your mind." However, we have also found that sin intervenes, cutting us off from him; for as the Psalmist says, "There is none righteous, no not one" (Ps 14.1–3). But finally, we should notice that the Law continues to play a positive role even within the context of redemption, as the Apostle Paul attempts to explain in the seventh chapter of Romans:

> What shall we say then? Is the Law sin? May it never be! *On the contrary, I would not have come to know sin except through the Law; for I would not have known about coveting if the Law had not said, "You shall not covet."* But sin, taking opportunity through the commandment, produced in me coveting of every kind; for apart from the Law sin is dead. And I was once alive apart from the law; but when the commandment came, sin became alive, and I died; and this commandment, which was to result in life, proved to result in death for

me; for sin, taking opportunity through the commandment, deceived me, and through it killed me. *So then, the Law is holy, and the commandment is holy and righteous and good. Therefore did that which is good become a cause of death for me? May it never be! Rather it was sin, in order that it might be shown to be sin effecting my death through that which was good,* that through the commandment sin might become utterly sinful (Rom 7.7–13).

Paul reminds us that the Law has a positive purpose, calling our attention to the righteousness of God and to our need to establish a positive relationship with him. However, he also insists that sin separates us from God, and this fact prevents the Law from accomplishing its positive purpose. But what then is the Law's derivative task? Paul tells us that its purpose is to bring us face to face with ourselves and to force us to face our sinful predicament. As a result, we cannot lay the Law aside, even within the context of grace, for it calls our attention to the righteousness of God. And we cannot lay it aside in the second place because it forces us to face our fragmentation so that we can become receptive to the grace of God. Thus Paul concludes his argument in verses twenty-four and twenty-five of this same chapter by saying: "Wretched man that I am! Who will set me free from the body of this death? Thanks be to God through Jesus Christ our Lord!" (Rom 7.24,25). Jesus, speaking many years before to his disciples, cautions them not to annul the power of the Law, and he does so because it is the Law that brings the fragmented soul to the threshold of God's kingdom. Moreover, he warns the disciples that if they blunt the power of the Law to accomplish this purpose, their own status in the kingdom will be inversely proportional to their consequent failure to make it accessible to others.

The summary of this entire discussion and of the theological significance reflected in it is to be found in verse twenty of the fifth chapter of Matthew, where Jesus says: "For I say unto you, that unless your righteousness surpasses that of the scribes and Pharisees, you shall not enter the kingdom of heaven" (Mt 5.20). There are three kinds of righteousness which are relevant to this passage and which must be clearly distinguished. In the first place, there is the righteousness of the Law, which was the kind of righteousness that fascinated the religious leaders in the first instance. They saw that the purpose of the Law was to bring us into a positive relationship with God, and as a result, they called the Law "righteous." But having acknowledged the righteousness of the Law, they began to be preoccupied with their own righteousness, and it is thus the righteousness of the scribes and Pharisees to which Jesus refers directly in this verse.

How was the scholarly preoccupation with one's own righteousness expressed? The Law, righteous as it was, was intended to make God accessible. But as scholars attempted to interpret it, they found that detailed and almost endless reflection was required. What, precisely, should one do on the Sabbath day? And how are the restrictions that govern fasting and purification to be formulated? The interpreters concluded that a set of commentaries was required to overcome the inherent vagueness of the Law. But what happened when they were seated at the scribal table? The attention of the scribes was often turned away from the righteousness of the Law to a righteousness of their own making, which generated what Jesus called "the tradition of men" and which of course is righteousness of a degenerate kind.

In the third place Jesus points by implication to the most fundamental kind of righteousness which he wants his followers to understand—namely, the righteousness of God that is made accessible to them in spite of their sin. As we have indicated already, righteousness of this kind comes to its fullest expression when Jesus brings the Law and the Prophets to fulfillment in his own life and work. The Law, then, positive as it was in the first instance, but degenerate as it became in scholarly hands, turns us by implication to the righteousness of God which makes access to God's kingdom possible. It is this kind of righteousness that exceeds the righteousness of the scribes and the Pharisees, for it is righteousness of this kind that is grounded in the grace of God.

> However, the Law itself must be preserved, even within the context of grace, for it not only calls our attention to the righteousness of God, but also confronts us with our own fragmentation and makes it possible for us to respond to the righteousness God wishes to bestow upon his followers.

CHAPTER VII

MURDER AND ANGER

❦

In the seventeenth verse of the fifth chapter of Matthew, Jesus says: "Do not think that I came to abolish the Law and the Prophets; I did not come to abolish, but to fulfill." This claim is no doubt intended to call the attention of his audience to the value and the dignity of their origins and to point to the religious significance of the context out of which the Hebrew tradition had emerged. Yet in claiming that he has come to bring the Law and the Prophets to fulfillment, Jesus suggests that the past must not only be preserved, but must also be taken to a higher level of self-realization. Jesus claims that this higher level is to be achieved in his own life and work, where we find an expression of grace that will make fellowship with God possible. The Law calls our attention to the righteousness of God, demanding that we love him with all our being and that we love our neighbors as ourselves. Yet sin intervenes and generates an infinite chasm between ourselves and the One we are asked to obey, making it impossible for us to measure up to the Law's requirements. The Law itself also degenerates in scholarly hands, for the scholar is preoccupied with interpretations of the Law that become an impossible burden, and which tempt us to embrace the self-righteousness that often results from obedience to a host of derivative requirements. In claiming that he has come to bring the Law and the Prophets to fulfillment, Jesus gives us access to the righteousness of God and makes it possible for the righteousness of his followers to exceed the righteousness of the scribes and Pharisees.

Jesus called his followers to embrace a new way of life, and in Chapter Five he emphasizes the novelty of the new world into which he wishes to lead them by introducing a formula that resonates throughout the remainder of the chapter. In this formula Jesus says: "You have heard that it was said . . . , but I say to you . . ." (Mt 5.21–48). In the earlier passage where he claims that he has not come to destroy but to fulfill the Law, Jesus emphasizes the continuity of the past and the future, suggesting that he intends to bring the religious origins of his audience to a consummation in his own life and work. However, this new formula points to a radical discontinuity between the past and the future, allowing Jesus to emphasize the positive content of his revolutionary teaching.

This new teaching focuses upon five practical problems which he asks his followers to consider, each of which is dealt with in terms of the formula that distinguishes the traditional teaching from the message of the new kingdom. The first of these issues is the problem of murder and anger; the second, the problem of adultery and divorce; the third, the problem of false oaths; the fourth, the problem of revenge; and the fifth, the problem of loving one's enemies. Jesus deals with all of these problems by comparing the Law and the commentaries upon it with the new way of life he intends to make accessible. However, the most crucial fact about his way of dealing with these problems is that he brings human relationships into the center of his teaching. As we have discovered already, the Sermon on the Mount is cosmic in its implications: it goes inside to the poor in spirit; it goes outside to those who hunger and thirst; it moves backward to the past and has something to say about the Law; it drives forward toward a new world, reaching to its very rim; and it reaches up to God himself, giving us access to divine happiness, and allowing us to become citizens of God's kingdom. This section of the Sermon focuses upon the human realm and upon the concrete relationships in which we are asked to stand in the light of the grace of God. Thus, beginning with verse twenty-one and continuing to the end of Chapter Five, we find the human being, the sanctity of the person, and the absolute centrality of human relationships brought to the center of our attention.[1]

I remember how as a young man I first learned something about the importance of the human being and about the centrality of human

relationships for the Christian community. Philosophers are not inclined to make human personality the center of their reflections, and
abstract speculation does not usually regard human relationships as
the really vital thing. However, for two summers I studied with a
psychologist who was trained in the psychology of religion, but who
was also the chaplain of a hospital, performing all the duties appropriate to that role. I remember clearly how he dealt with the typical
philosophical mentality. He was not especially interested to hear the
contents of my latest speculative endeavors, though I was very eager
to communicate them to him. Instead, he urged me to go out onto the
hospital floor, go into the rooms of the patients, *listen to what they said,*
try to say as little as possible, and then come back to the office to write
down in a verbatum report what had transpired in the conversation. I
went out to the floor, I went to the rooms, I listened, I tried to talk as
little as possible, I came back to write down the results and, of course,
those verbatum reports became the context in which my speculations
began to develop again—ruminations about the problem of sickness,
thoughts about the problem of death, reflections about the relevance
of Christianity to the human predicament, and so on. My teacher kept
handing them back and asking, "Where is the *person* you spoke with in
what you have written? Where is the authentic voice of the individual
you visited to be found here?" Slowly, over a period of two summers,
I began to understand this central theme: If the religious dimension of
experience is to be taken seriously, it must come to focus on the human
realm, upon the human personality, and upon the interactions that
occur between human beings in the light of the grace of God.

A particular episode, I recall, finally made the crucial point inescapable. I was called up to the fifth floor of the hospital where a patient
had become hysterical in one of the larger hospital wards. Though I
was the understudy, the nurse no doubt assumed that after two summers I had learned enough to be able to deal with the situation. When I
arrived the problem was compounded, for the patient sensed that I
was approaching her situation from my own point of view and was
responding to her predicament in essentially theoretical terms. As her
violence intensified, and as my own incapacity to respond appropriately became more evident, the nurse called the chaplain, asking for
his help. Ten minutes later he strolled into the room, walked up to the

patient, put his hand on her shoulder, and as they walked down the hall to an empty room I heard him say as the door shut, "What is your name?" Ten minutes later, they came out; she walked over to her bed, lay down, and said to him, "I will take my medicine now." As my teacher and I walked back to the office, a single thought finally crystalized: "What we are doing here has something to do with somebody's name, and what we say must speak directly to the human situation."

In the Sermon on the Mount, Jesus speaks in cosmic terms, but as he turns to the center of his message he also addresses us in human terms, bringing the centrality of human relationships to the focus of our attention. Notice how he formulates the crucial point in verses twenty-one and twenty-two:

> You have heard that the ancients were told, "You shall not commit murder" and "Whoever commits murder shall be liable to the court." But I say to you that everyone who is angry with his brother shall be guilty before the court; and whoever shall say to his brother, "Raca," shall be guilty before the supreme court; and whoever shall say, "You fool," shall be guilty enough to go into the [hell of fire] (Mt 5.21,22).

Let us focus on verse twenty-one and the first clause of verse twenty-two. First, Jesus reminds his disciples of the familiar proscription against murder. Exodus 20:13 does not say "Thou shall not kill" but, instead, "Thou shall not commit murder" (Ex 20.13); and in Exodus 21:12 the same Lawgiver says, "If someone commits a murder, he shall be put to death" (Ex 21.12). The context of the discussion has to do, not with killing as such, but with murdering someone; and it is murder that Jesus has in mind when he first reminds his disciples about the traditional teaching. But characteristically and more fundamentally, Jesus moves further by saying, "Having heard the familiar commandment against murder, I have something fresh and absolutely revolutionary to teach you; and that new teaching is not only that you shall not commit murder, but that you must not be angry with your brother, for even if you do this second thing, you will be guilty before the court."

The most obvious question to ask about this passage is why the prohibition against murder is extended to the problem of anger, and as we should perhaps expect, part of the answer is to be found by focusing upon the meaning of the word in question. *Orgizo* is the word for "anger" in this case, and it means not those momentary fits of anger that come upon us unexpectedly, but the *smoldering, festering cauldron within* from which violent action springs. Having reminded his audience that they must not commit murder, he also tells them that they must avoid the kind of anger that smolders until it sometimes explodes; for even if the explosion *never* occurs, we will be guilty before the court because of the anger itself. And this is so, first because the seething anger *will* overflow, if not in murder, in other ways; and in the second place, because anger of this kind will destroy the soul in which the anger itself occurs.

Being guilty before the court is being called to account for the disruption of the human soul which sometimes expresses itself overtly and which, when it is kept within, points to the fragmentation of the human realm. Thus Jesus says, "The ancients said, 'Do not commit murder' " —and there is vital social significance in that thesis. But in the second place, lurking behind the overt act is *the attitude* and, indeed, *the fragmentation* of the consciousness that engages in the act, which is far more fundamental and which will be destructive beyond measure, both toward others and toward the one in whom the initial anger wells up. We should not be surprised, then, that Jesus says, "If this occurs, you will be guilty before the court." *Who* is going to pay the penalty for the smoldering, erupting, angry consciousness? No doubt those whom we encounter, but in a certain way and far more fundamentally, the person in whom the anger itself is to be found. Jesus reminds us of the past when he refers to the prohibition against murder, but then shifts our attention to a new teaching with respect to the problem of anger.

Notice how he develops this theme in the second clause of verse twenty-two: "and whoever shall say to his brother, 'Raca,' shall be guilty before the supreme court," that is to say, before the Sanhedrin council. The crucial word in the text that is merely transliterated is an Aramaic expression that corresponds to the *sound* a person makes as he clears his throat before he spits in someone's face. The term is left untranslated to allow this negative characteristic of the act in question to remain evident. But who are the people in whose faces we are most likely to spit? They are most likely one of two kinds: either someone below us for whom we have contempt; or someone very close to us to whom we react violently out of self-contempt. In the first case, we respond to someone below us whom we despise, while in the second case, we react to one so close to us that we spit in his face as a way of spitting in our own. Notice that Jesus is talking about our 'brothers' here, and by implication, about people within what will soon become the Christian community he is asking his disciples to generate. Thus he says, "In that new community, you must move past murder to the source of it, and you must deal with the bubbling cauldron within. And in the second place, you must not spit in the face of another, for if you do so, you will be guilty before the highest court." Spitting in a person's face reaches either to the depths or to the heights; it reaches below us or it reaches out to someone very close to us and, indeed, turns back upon ourselves; and when this occurs, the only place to find judgment is in the highest court, for a violation of this kind reaches to the very center of human existence.

There is one further step to be found in the last clause of verse twenty-two, where Jesus says, "and whoever shall say, 'You fool,' shall be guilty enough to go into the hell of fire." At this point, Jesus does not simply speak about anger, or about spitting in someone's face, but also warns us against calling another person "a fool." But why does this third stage of the argument lead to the radical degeneration to which the concept of Hell calls our attention? The very simple response is that to use this expression of another is to dehumanize the person completely. The Psalmist tells us that the fool has said in his heart, "There is no God" (Ps 14.1). Being a fool and denying God's existence are very closely linked both in Scripture and in the subsequent philosophical commentary upon it. Augustine makes a great deal of the relationship between being foolish and failing to acknowledge the existence of God; and he quotes the Psalmist to the effect that *it is the fool who is finally cut off from God.*[2] Why? Because he is cut off from the ground of his existence, and his foolishness consists in the fact that his life is fragmented at the center. In this verse Jesus suggests that when we call another a fool, we not only dehumanize the person, but also imply that he has lost touch with the meaning of human existence. The Psalmist tells us that the fool is cut off from God. If I say, then, to another, "Thou fool," I say by implication: "You are not only beneath contempt, but you are also utterly separated from the foundation of human existence."

Notice once more the pattern of Jesus' discussion in verses twenty-one and twenty-two: he not only reminds us that we should not commit murder, but also tells us to avoid the kind of smoldering anger that results in the indirect killing of another, and in the direct killing of one's self. Furthermore, he tells us not to spit in someone else's face because whether he is lower than we or very close to us the act itself reflects our fragmented condition. Finally, he warns us not to call someone a fool, for when we do, we are implying that the person in question is utterly cut off from the ground of human existence. Calling another a fool is a way of denying the ultimate significance of the person to whom the remark is addressed. But what is the consequence in the case of calling another a fool? On this occasion, Jesus does not simply refer to the court, or to the highest court in the land, but speaks instead about "the hell of fire." The literal expression used is the "Valley of Hinnom," or "Gehenna," as it is sometimes rendered. The Valley of Hinnom was outside Jerusalem and was the place where the refuse was deposited only to be left burning and smoldering. The smoldering condition of that valley is a picture of the soul that has first been angry, then spit in the face of his brother, and finally said to another, "Thou fool, you are utterly cut off from God." When I make an utterance of this kind, I stand in the smoldering predicament where the garbage is to be found, and where the refuse will simply continue to burn.[3]

Let us notice how Jesus continues to develop the discussion in verses twenty-three and twenty-four:

> If therefore you are presenting your offering at the altar, and there remember that your brother has something against you, leave your offering there before the altar, and go your way; first be reconciled to your brother, and then come and present your offering (Mt 5.23, 24).

Jesus is apparently speaking here about the same person we have offended in verses twenty-one and twenty-two, and he is also still addressing the ones who are angry, those who spit in the face of another, and those who say to another "Thou fool." For what do we do after we have stood in all three of those places? We sometimes enter a place of worship, expecting that coming to the altar will somehow remedy the defects described in such detail in the earlier passage.

Before they were able to offer a sacrifice at the altar, the Jews were required to do two things: first they had to bathe, and then they had to change their clothes. I take it that this passage still has contemporary relevance. Having expressed the explosive anger of verses twenty-one and twenty-two, one response is to flee—both from ourselves and from our predicament—and one place to turn is to the place of worship where we wash our hands, change our clothes, and approach the sacrificial altar where the offering is about to be given. However, as we approach the altar, we sometimes remember the content of the earlier verses, and when this occurs, Jesus says: "Leave your gift at the altar, go out into the street, be reconciled with your brother, and then come back to the altar so that the vertical relation being pointed to there can be re-established in all its richness."

What should we do when we leave our gift at the altar in order to be reconciled with our brother, and how should the reconciliation process unfold? It need not take the form of a long discussion. Sometimes long discussions with alienated neighbors make the alienation worse! The longer we talk, the more self-indulgent the discussion becomes, and the more we prolong the encounter, the more intent we become upon reliving the predicament instead of recovering the source of power that will take us back to the altar. However, there are two prescriptions in the Scripture about how to deal with the problem of reconciliation, each of which can be brought to bear upon our present condition. In I John 1:9, the writer says, "If we confess our sins, He is faithful and just to forgive us our sins, and to cleanse us from all unrighteousness." The word "confess" means simply: "To acknowledge what we have done." Now if these instructions, which refer primarily to our relation with God, are also brought to bear upon our relations with others, the prescription asks us to say: "I have offended you, and I want to acknowledge what I have done." We can spare the person being addressed the crying we might do in private, and we can spare ourselves that. It might very well be that the richest possible discussion can develop; it might be that it cannot, or that it might not even be necessary. But the first thing necessary is to say to the person we have offended, "I want to confess to you what I have done."

A second prescription about how to deal with the problem of reconciliation is to be found in the third chapter of Philippians, verses thirteen and fourteen. Paul has just expressed pride in his Jewish heritage, but has also confessed that he has persecuted the church, pointing by implication to those he had imprisoned and to others he had martyred, and suggesting the extent to which he despised himself by describing himself later as "the greatest of sinners" (1 Tm 1.15). But what does Paul say when he reaches the climax of his account in the third chapter of Philippians? He says:

> Brethen, I do not regard myself as having laid hold of it yet; but one thing I do: forgetting what lies behind and reaching forward to what lies ahead, I press on toward the goal for the prize of the upward call of God in Christ Jesus (Phil 3.13,14).

First, we must confess our sins and say to those whom we have offended, "This is what I have done"; and then as Paul suggests, we must forget what lies behind in order to re-establish a positive relationship with God. Of course, this is easier said than done. The more verbal we are, the more likely we are to dwell on the problem explicitly; and the less verbal we are, the more we are likely to smolder within. However, from a spiritual as well as a psychological point of view, the New Testament speaks directly to our predicament. It tells us that if we have brought our gift to the altar, and if we remember that another person has something against us, we must first confess our sins and then forget them. For only then will it be possible for us to return to the altar and re-enter the vertical realm where divine righteousness is to be found.

Let us now turn to verses twenty-five and twenty-six, where

Jesus brings his discussion of this first practical problem to a conclusion. In this passage, he says:

> Make friends quickly with your opponent at law while you are with him on the way, in order that your opponent may not deliver you to the judge, and the judge to the officer, and you be thrown into prison. Truly I say to you, you shall not come out of there, until you have paid up the last cent (Mt 5.25,26).

In the previous four verses, Jesus has been speaking about our relation to our brothers, and about the need to establish reconciliation in this context in the face of the anger and hostility that sometimes erupt. However, in this passage, he takes us back to the larger world, speaking in this context not about our brother but about our adversary.

The context in which Jesus spoke was an agricultural economy, and enemies within that kind of economy were often made in the following way: A farmer borrows the money to plant his crops—just as farmers do today; in the meantime, a dispute arises between the farmer who has borrowed the money and someone he meets in the course of the day; the person knows that he has had to borrow money for his seed, so he goes to the lender, buys up the note, and then goes back to the farmer who has borrowed the money and forecloses on the note before the harvest comes and he has had time to pay his debt. The kind of adversary Jesus has in mind could very well be encountered in a situation like this. But what is the farmer to do in a situation of this kind? Jesus says, "Make friends quickly," for otherwise he will be thrown into prison and will not escape until his debt is paid in full. But what are the conditions for making friends quickly with an adversary? And how can friendship emerge from a context of conflict? The only way this can occur is for us to reach out to our adversary in a gratuitous act of reconciliation.

Philia derives from agape, especially when reconciliation is to be established between those who are enemies. Thus, we encounter our adversary in the street—not now our brother and not the one we have offended and have attempted to reconcile before we return to the altar, but this time an enemy who is prepared to call us to account because of our debts. What is Jesus' advice? Make friends quickly, and the quickest way to do this is to respond to our enemies with the same kind of gratuitous act that God himself has displayed toward the world. When this occurs, Jesus claims that friendship can flourish; but notice also that when friendship flourishes, there will be a further consequence: we will not have to pay the last cent before the judgment bar of the Law. When one responds to the adversary with the gratuitous act of agape that makes friendship possible, he is set free from the binding tentacles of the Law.

It is possible to read this verse simply in pragmatic terms: Jesus tells his followers that they must make friends with their adversary quickly if they are to avoid the punishment that will follow from a failure to do so. But is the Sermon on the Mount not also saying something more? When we confront our enemies with agape so that friendship can flourish, the power of the Law is broken. Moreover, when the power of the Law is broken, the righteousness of God is made accessible, and the penalty that would have to be paid because of the Law is transcended once more by a divine gift.

CHAPTER VIII

ADULTERY AND DIVORCE

❧

In our study of the fifth chapter of Matthew, we have found that Jesus uses two phrases to characterize his relation to the past. The first of these phrases occurs in verse seventeen where he says, "Do not think that I came to abolish the Law and the Prophets; I did not come to abolish, but to fulfill." The fundamental purpose of the Law was to make fellowship with God possible, and at least part of what Jesus intends to suggest in this passage is that the sin that separates us from Him is to be overcome in his own life and work. Jesus fulfills the past by giving us access to the One whom the Law and the Prophets originally attempted to make accessible. However, Jesus also uses a second phrase to distinguish himself from the past and to characterize the uniqueness of his teaching. As he says on five separate occasions in verses twenty-one through forty-eight, "You have heard that it has been said . . . , but I say unto you. . . ." Having reaffirmed the past, Jesus also wants to move beyond it, and he does so by addressing five practical problems that are to be found at the center of the human realm. For example, he reaffirms the Old Testament prohibition against murder, but he also tells us that the root of the problem is to be found in the anger that wells up from within, forcing us to confront the fragmented consciousness from which interpersonal discord often emerges. Jesus therefore plunges into the center of a practical problem to which the Law and the Prophets had attempted to address themselves.

One of the most important implications of Jesus' revolutionary teaching is that his words serve to bring us all under judgment. We can perhaps regard the prohibition against murder as having very little personal significance, but it is much harder to evade the existential import of those other utterances: "Do not be angry; do not spit in the face of another; and never call another person a fool." Thus, the words of Jesus not only serve to take the Old Testament tradition to a higher level, but also move us into the heart of the human predicament, forcing us to confront hidden dimensions of our existence from which we might otherwise be tempted to turn away. The words of Jesus not only bring his audience under judgment, but bring the commentators on the Sermon on the Mount under judgment as well. In these three chapters Jesus moves in so many directions that it is virtually impossible to be adequate to his intentions in their rich, full-bodied complexity. He speaks about the inside of the person, only in the next sentence to talk about our relation to the larger world; he insists on the primacy of the human personality and of human relationships when he talks about murder and anger, but at the same time he calls our attention to our relationship with God, against the backdrop of which all the rest of his discussion receives its significance. On the surface, the Sermon on the Mount appears to be relatively simple and straightforward, but in fact, it proves to be an exegetical land mine, pointing simultaneously in many different directions. The hermeneutical stumbling block with respect to the text is the temptation to read it exclusively in terms of only one of the themes upon which Jesus wishes to focus our attention. However, the fundamental task of the commentator is to read and be judged by all the dimensions of Jesus' message—the inner, the outer, the past, the future, the human, and the divine—richly interwoven.

One of the central questions which the deceptive simplicity of the Sermon on the Mount forces us to ask is this: "Where can principles of interpretation be found that will serve to lead us through what might otherwise become an inaccessible labyrinth?" There are two places in Scripture where the clearest guidance is to be found as we approach the Sermon on the Mount. The first is in the words of Jesus himself in the twenty-second chapter of Matthew which we have considered already. In that passage, Jesus summarizes the earlier teaching of the Law and the Prophets in two familiar sayings: first, love God with all your heart; and in the second place, love your neighbor as yourself. If we could write those two utterances across the Sermon on the Mount as the key for uncovering its significance, much of what would otherwise be impenetrable would begin to fall into place. Those two dimensions point toward God and also toward the larger world, but most interpretations run aground because of their failure to come to focus on both of them simultaneously. The Sermon is read either as a humanistic document designed to chart the ethical course of civilization—in which case God drops away—or as a message intended only for a small group of devout followers, depriving it of its relevance to the real world and to the tangled interpersonal relationships in which all of us stand. However, Jesus himself suggests that if we focus both on God and on our neighbor, we can never get away from the vertical dimension, on the one hand, or the horizontal thrust of the message on the other. Thus, our first hermeneutical principle for approaching Jesus' message is one that places both God and our neighbor at the center of our attention.

There is also a second passage of Scripture in the sixth chapter of Proverbs which can serve to give us an indication of the thrust of Jesus' teaching in the Sermon on the Mount. In Proverbs, Chapter Six, verses sixteen through nineteen, the writer says:

> There are six things which the Lord hates, yes, seven which are an abomination to Him: haughty eyes, a lying tongue, and hands that shed innocent blood, a heart that devises wicked plans, feet that run rapidly toward evil, a false witness who utters lies, and one who spreads strife among his brothers (Prv 6.16–19).

We have spoken already about murder in the previous chapter, but though it appears in this list, the important thing to notice about the passage as a whole is that it focuses primarily on sins of the heart. In fact, at the very center of the passage in question we find the phrase, "a heart that devises wicked plans." If God himself stands behind the Sermon on the Mount, and if the importance of interpersonal relationships also comes to focus in Jesus' teaching, we also find there the sins of Proverbs 6, the central one of which suggests that the problem of sin at its most fundamental level *is a problem of the heart.*

What, then, does Jesus wish to convey by interlacing all of these themes in his message? Presumably, he wants to suggest that there is a vertical dimension of experience without which the Sermon on the Mount is an utterly meaningless document. Whatever humanistic comfort might be derived from the message pales into insignificance by comparison with the richness it acquires when it is anchored in the love for God that is in turn dependent upon God's grace. In the second place, there is a horizontal dimension that has to do with our relations with our neighbors, and which accounts in large measure for the detailed content of the Sermon. Jesus does not speak in abstractions but speaks instead about murder and anger, adultery and divorce, the problem of false oaths, the problem of revenge, and the problem of loving our enemies. In fact, throughout the Sermon, we find a network of interpersonal relationships interwoven with the vertical thrust of the message.

Finally, when we ask why it is necessary for Jesus to preach a sermon of this kind, we find that the answer is to be found in the fact that sin separates us from God. If Jesus' first words are love God and love your neighbor, the intervening word becomes, "I have difficulty doing that; and in fact, it is utterly impossible for me to do so out of my own resources because I am cut off from God, and I am separated from my neighbor." Jesus would not have demanded that we love God and love our neighbor if we were not confronted by the problem of sin. He suggests throughout his message that the problem of sin is not located primarily in our overt interactions with one another, but is to be found, instead, in the heart. Therefore, the fourfold theme—God, the neighbor, sin, and the divided heart—echoes in an interwoven pattern throughout the whole of Jesus' teaching.

This reference to sins of the heart lays the foundation for our discussion of the second practical problem that Jesus considers, for as Jesus tells us in verses twenty-seven and twenty-eight of Chapter Five:

> You have heard that it was said, "You shall not commit adultery";
> but I say to you, that everyone who looks on a woman to lust for

her has committed adultery with her already in his heart (Mt
5.27,28).

In discussing this passage, it is important to notice that some of his
contemporaries who were so sharply critical of Jesus' teaching were
often preoccupied with the problem of adultery and that the details
of his discussion are determined by this fact. The sin of adultery is an
overt act that is relatively easily understandable; it is concerned not
with what goes on behind the veil of one's own fragmented consciousness but with its external manifestations; and the Mosaic law
clearly prescribed that the act in question be punished by stoning the
guilty party to death. But what does Jesus say about the issue in his
own right, having acknowledged the importance of the problem in
its original Mosaic form? He says that the real problem is not *the act*
of verse twenty-seven, but *the glance* of verse twenty-eight that expresses the *adulterous intention of the heart* with which the verse concludes. The word "looks at" in the text is a translation of *blepo,*
which means "to catch a glimpse out of the corner of one's eye." As a
result, we may re-translate verses twenty-seven and twenty-eight as
follows: "You have heard that it was said, 'You shall not commit
adultery'; but I say to you, whoever glances at a woman to lust after
her has already committed adultery in his heart." Thus Jesus turns
our attention once more from the external world to the unfocused
center of human existence.

What in more detail was the typical attitude toward the problem
of adultery which has a special bearing on Jesus' teaching? Religious
leaders were not engaged in committing it; they were very preoccupied with it; they were quick to punish it; but finally, they were not
prepared to give an account of the intentions of their hearts, for
surrounding the religious consciousness was a vacuum seal of self-
righteousness. The context Jesus confronted can therefore be described in the following way: here is the overt act, here is the preoccupation with it, here is the willingness to punish it severely by
stoning, and here is the self-righteous soul; let us confront the lustful
heart hidden there; and let us finally locate the source of the problem of
adultery in the fragmented soul. If therefore we punish another for
committing adultery when lust is surging within, we will in the very

act of punishment be brought to judgment for the twisted condition of
our own souls.

There is of course a classic story about Jesus' way of dealing
with the problem of adultery to be found at the beginning of the
eighth chapter of John. John tells us that when Jesus came into the
temple early one morning:

> The scribes and the Pharisees brought a woman caught in adultery,
> and having set her in the midst, they said to Him, "Teacher, this
> woman has been caught in adultery, in the very act. Now in the
> Law Moses commanded us to stone such women; what then do
> You say?" And they were saying this, testing Him, in order that
> they might have grounds for accusing him (Jn 8.2–6).

We have already found that the phrase, "you have heard that it was
said . . . , but I say unto you . . . ," echoes throughout the Sermon
on the Mount. In this interchange as it is recorded in John's gospel
that same antithesis is formulated with respect to a particular inci-
dent, and indeed, in even more personal and arresting terms. Here
the Pharisees say, "In the Law Moses commanded us to stone such
women; what then do you say?" Jesus' answer to this pointed question can therefore be brought to bear upon the same problem as it
presents itself in the Sermon on the Mount.

It is important to notice that in answering the question, Jesus
does not fasten his attention primarily upon the overt act, nor upon
the woman who committed it, nor even upon the law violated in the
act itself, but upon the surrounding Pharisees who had brought the
episode to his attention. Jesus knows, and he wants his audience to
know, that the problem of sin is primarily a problem of the fragmented heart. Thus, he addresses the Pharisees first by stooping
down and writing with his finger in the sand, and when they ignore
what he has written and persist in asking their urgent question, he
stands up and says to them, "He who is without sin among you, let
him be the first to throw a stone at her" (Jn 8.6,7). Thus Jesus
attempts to turn their attention away from the overt act of adultery
to the deepest recesses of their own souls, for it is there that the
problem of sin must finally be addressed. Jesus returns to the overt

act in his later discussion with the woman, but at this point he chooses to focus on the problem of sin as a problem of the heart. And he does this once more by stooping down and by writing in the sand.

There have been a number of interesting conjectures about what Jesus wrote on the ground. Perhaps he wrote the Ten Commandments, for if he did, love for God and love for one's neighbor were made central in what he had to say. But suppose he also wrote Proverbs 6, verses sixteen through nineteen, which comes to focus on the twisted heart? In either case, it is not surprising that John tells us in verse nine of Chapter Eight that "when they heard it, they began to go out one by one, beginning with the older ones, and He was left alone, and the woman, where she had been, in the midst." It is only when the Pharisees have gone that Jesus addresses the woman directly. And he says simply, "Woman, where are they? Did no one condemn you?" And she said, "No one, Lord." And Jesus said, "Neither do I condemn you; go your way. From now on sin no more" (Jn 8.10,11).

Of course, Jesus' remark to the woman does not imply that he simply excused her. The word "comdemnation" means "utter separation from God." Therefore, Jesus' remark implies that he is not prepared to call the woman a fool, or to suggest that she is utterly cut off from God. In fact, he does not even mention her sin until he has first talked about grace, for grace not only outstrips the Law, but it also outstrips sin. The first word from God is about the grace of God; the first word of Jesus to the Pharisees is about the distorted heart that separates us from it; and the first word of Jesus to the woman is about forgiveness that can even conquer condemnation. It is only after grace has done its work that Jesus tells the woman to sin no more. Unfortunately, the men who are preoccupied with the problem of adultery have already gone away, unforgiven for their failure to notice the implication of their glances, and separated in their own self-righteousness from the redemptive grace of God.

In discussing the problem of adultery, it is illuminating to remember that at the time of Jesus, there was a Jewish sect called the "bleeding Pharisees."[1] They were called "bleeding Pharisees" because they so dreaded the possibility of adultery that they wore blindfolds, causing them to stumble in the streets until their heads and bodies bled. In addressing Pharisees of this kind in verse twenty-eight, Jesus therefore says by implication, "Get your heads up, and take the blinders off! The problem of adultery is not primarily in the act, or even in the glance, but in the self-righteous intention of the lustful heart." It is not possible to deal with the problem of adultery with a blindfold, for if we attempt to do so, two questions inevitably arise: first, "What are we thinking about when we place the blindfold on our heads, and in the second place, what will happen when the blindfold slips and we catch a tempting glimpse out of the corner of our eye?" The answer to both questions is that those who are blindfolded are probably far more preoccupied with the problem of adultery than those who commit the act. The "bleeding Pharisees" wore blindfolds to be certain that the problem of adultery would never arise. However, with the blindfold in place, they still had time to think, and when the blindfold slipped, the glance to which Jesus refers easily issued in a lustful heart. Therefore, Jesus says that the chief problem to be addressed is not the problem of adultery itself, but the problem generated by the turmoil of adultery in the heart.

Let me now attempt to address the problem before us in even more direct and straightforward terms. Is it ever possible for us to live without responding to other human beings in sexual terms, either overt or covert? Or is it possible for us to deal with one another without the sexual dimension of experience being a crucial aspect of the interaction? I very much doubt it, and there is no reason why one should. That is not what Jesus is concerned with here. He does not suggest that we must deal with others in a fashion that never has sexual implications. What he *is* concerned about, however, is that this way of dealing with one another not become the focal preoccupation of existence so that the glance or the look degenerates into the embroiled inner condition which he refers to in the middle of verse twenty-eight as lust, and which issues in what he calls the adulterous heart. There is a radical difference between dealing with one another in terms appropriate to our sexuality—which is presumably part of our created condition which God declared to be good—and the distortions from which Jesus is attempting to lead us. In fact, he focuses his attention upon those whose solution to the problem of sexuality was to put on a blindfold, suggesting that the problem was not to avoid temptation, but to deal with one another in sexual terms without degeneration. Of course, Jesus knows that a glance will sometimes produce sexual thoughts, and he also knows that thoughts of this kind will sometimes issue in action that is inappropriate. However, he does not focus on this dimension of the issue, but rather upon the lustful heart with which verse twenty-eight concludes. Jesus is concerned with the fragmentation of the human soul and wishes to denounce the religious consciousness that explodes because it "has committed adultery in its heart."

In verses twenty-nine and thirty of Chapter Five, Jesus continues his attack upon some of his contemporaries by proposing a radical remedy for the problem of the lustful heart. In this passage he says:

> And if your right eye makes you stumble, tear it out, and throw it from you; for it is better for you that one of the parts of your body perish, than for your whole body to be thrown into hell. And if your right hand makes you stumble, cut it off, and throw it from you; for it is better for you that one of the parts of your body perish, than for your whole body to go into hell (Mt 5.29,30).

This passage is directed once more to those who attempted to deal with the problem of adultery by using blindfolds, and it is clearly an instance of hyperbolic teaching. In proposing a radical remedy for the adultery in one's heart, Jesus not only suggests that we take off our blindfolds, but demands that we remove our eye and hand as well! Hyperbolic teaching is a rhetorical attempt to capture the attention of an audience through deliberate exaggeration, and Jesus does so here by suggesting that it would be better for those who must use blindfolds to carry that remedy to its natural conclusion in an even more radical form. Moreover, he claims that it would be better for the body to be dismembered than for the entire person to be separated from God.

The focus of Jesus' teaching is the centered self, and anything that prevents us from standing in a vertical relation with God must simply be discarded. It may involve great pain to reach the place where one's fragmented existence is made whole, and some dimensions of our natural consciousness might need to be discarded along the way. However, the crucial point is that the vertical relation with God be established and that anything that prevents it be quickly eliminated. Lust is one of the features of the human psyche that can easily masquerade as ultimate, and this is so because the passionate intensity involved can easily be mistaken for the centered self. Lust can turn us away from God because of its power, and it is one of the few things powerful enough to displace what is ultimate with a surrogate form of itself. Jesus suggests that if we are consumed by lust and define our existence in these terms, this preliminary and degenerate self-definition must be discarded in the interest of what is genuinely ultimate. Thus Jesus suggests to the bleeding Pharisees that they not only discard their blindfolds, but an eye and limb as well, hoping in this way to call them back to a centered relationship with God.

Let us also notice at this point that there is another solution to the problem of sexuality that Jesus avoids which attempts to sublimate the lower dimensions of our nature into something higher. Jesus does not speak in that fashion here, nor does he even express an interest in sublimating what is lower into something higher. Rather, he is interested in bringing wholeness to the entire person—body, mind and spirit—and he attempts to do so by bringing all of these dimensions of the soul into a vertical relationship with God. The crucial metaphor is not "higher and lower," "subordination and subordinated," "sublimation of the lower into the higher," but the contrast between the centered self and the fragmentation into which human existence often falls. Jesus does not explain human wholeness in terms of sublimation, but in terms of the transformation of the fragmented self. As a result, his metaphors shift from the distinction between higher and lower to the contrast between the center and the periphery of human existence.

One way to emphasize this point is to notice that though Jesus speaks about dismemberment in graphic terms, he never says that dismemberment is necessary in order to enter the kingdom of God. Quite to the contrary, he simply suggests in hyperbolic terms that it might be required in exceptional circumstances.[2] Some religions suggest that dismemberment is not simply a religious possibility, but an absolute necessity. For example, if we construe the relationship between the spirit and the flesh as the relation between the soul and the body, and if we adopt the view that the soul must finally mutilate the body to rise to the heights, "dismemberment" is not simply a possibility in an extreme case, but a necessary condition for salvation. However, Jesus does not address embodied beings in order to force them to repudiate that side of their nature as a necessary condition for entering God's kingdom. If you believe that the sentence that says, "If your right hand or eye offend you, remove them and cast them from you in order to preserve the centered soul" is offensive, suppose he had said that we must do this in order to enter the kingdom of heaven? And suppose the implication of this injunction had been that the body is itself inherently negative, so that one must transcend it in order to have access to a higher realm? Then we would confront a radical but all too familiar teaching indeed, for it is a teaching of this kind that prevails in some religions until this day. However, this is *not* the teaching of Jesus. Jesus wants the person to be made whole, and he wants us to confront one another face to face as members of a transformed community. Therefore, he demands hyperbolically that lust be laid aside in the interest of developing a new kind of kingdom.

A final way to stress this point is to comment briefly on the fact that in discussing the possibility of dismemberment, Jesus mentions only the right eye and the right hand as requiring radical action. In appraising this fact, we should of course remember that most people in Jesus' day, as in ours, were right-handed, and that our natural orientation toward the world is determined by this fact. We reach out toward the world with our right eye and right hand, and the natural "tilt" of our being is determined by this fact. Thus Jesus says to his audience, "If a lustful heart is a problem that separates you from God and from your neighbor, the radical remedy for this predicament is to displace your 'natural' orientation toward the world with a unified and centered existence." And if it is the right eye and the right hand that offend us by fragmenting the soul, we must rid ourselves of them by bringing both God and our neighbor back to the center of our attention.

In considering the problem of the lustful heart, there is one final issue that Jesus discusses which is of particular inportance both then and now and which he formulates briefly in verses thirty-one and thirty-two:

> And it was said, "Whoever sends his wife away, let him give her a certificate of divorce"; but I say to you that everyone who divorces his wife, except for the cause of unchastity, makes her commit adultery; and whoever marries a divorced woman commits adultery (Mt 5.31,32).

In considering the significance of this passage, it is important to turn first to the Old Testament context to which Jesus refers, recorded in the twenty-fourth chapter of Deuteronomy, verses one through four:

> When a man takes a wife and marries her, and it happens that she finds no favor in his eyes because he has found some indecency in her, and he writes her a certificate of divorce and puts it in her hand and sends her out from his house, and she leaves his house and goes and becomes another man's wife, and if the latter husband turns against her and writes her a certificate of divorce and puts it in her hand and sends her out of his house, or if the latter husband dies who took her to be his wife, then her former husband who sent her away is not allowed to take her again to be his wife, since she has been defiled; for that is an abomination before the Lord, and you shall not bring sin on the land which the Lord your God gives you as an inheritance (Dt 24.1-4).

For the purposes of our discussion, the crucial part of this four-verse passage is the phrase "having found some indecency in her." Moses says that if a woman is found to be indecent after marriage, the husband can give her a certificate of divorce and dismiss her from his house. Thus, in interpreting the passage, everything hinges on what the term "indecency" or "uncleanliness" means.

In the twenty-second chapter of Deuteronomy, verses thirteen through twenty-one, we find a careful attempt to express what indecency means, and on the basis of this passage it is perfectly clear that what is in question is the matter of virginity. The situation in question is described in this way: After marriage occurs and the husband finds that his wife is not a virgin, he denounces her; and if it should prove to be the case that his denunciation is false, he is brought to judgment and must pay a penalty to the father of the misjudged bride. If, on the other hand, his allegation is correct, the woman is returned to the house of her father and is stoned to death. There is of course an obvious connection between these two passages as they pertain to the problem before us. In the twenty-fourth chapter of Deuteronomy, the certificate of divorce is mentioned, and a reference to uncleanliness occurs. And in the twenty-second chapter of that same book, the implication is that uncleanliness means intercourse before marriage, for which stoning is the penalty if the allegation proves to be correct. It is with reference to this context that Jesus is speaking when he considers the problem of divorce.

However, a problem arises when we attempt to reconcile these two passages, and this problem gives rise to a rabbinical dispute. The rabbi reasons that if uncleanliness in Deuteronomy 24 means what it apparently means in Deuteronomy 22, namely, unchastity, then the woman of Deuteronomy 24 would presumably have been stoned to death. But in this case the woman is given a certificate of dismissal when she is found to be unclean and is sent forth from the house. Thus, it must be that uncleanliness in Deuteronomy 24 does not mean simply what it means in Deuteronomy 22; for if it did, there would be no reason to give a certificate of divorce to a woman who was to be stoned to death. At the time of Jesus, the rabbinical schools therefore disagreed about the meaning of defilement in Deuteronomy 24. Shammai asserted that uncleanliness meant unchastity, and he explained the difference between Deuteronomy 22 and 24 in terms of the distinction between a loss of virginity prior to marriage and subsequent adultery. By contrast, Hillel asserted that uncleanliness does not simply mean unchastity, but any kind of uncleanliness whatever, even ceremonial.[3]

Of course, the Pharisees preferred this more liberal interpretation, for in terms of it, it was easy to dissolve the marriage contract. For example, there was a proscription against going into the house where a death had occurred, and if one of the Pharisees who had been so eager to stone the woman caught in adultery wished to divorce his wife, all that was required was that he arrange for her to enter the restricted house. When she returned, the Pharisee could then give her a certificate of dismissal, citing the ceremonial interpretation of Deuteronomy 24 as his excuse. Jesus of course understands this possibility, and as a result, he makes it clear to his followers that an easy divorce is not to be permitted to result from an unsettled rabbinical dispute. Thus Jesus asserts that divorce is not to be permitted except for the cause of unchastity, outflanking in this way the pharisaical mentality.

It is important to be clear about the fact that the reference to unchastity in the Sermon on the Mount has a polemical target, and that Jesus is intending to claim that a marriage is not to be dissolved for merely ceremonial reasons. The same person who places a blindfold on his head, and who is so preoccupied with adultery that he brings a woman caught in the act to Jesus simply to test his orthodoxy, is able to divorce his own wife on merely ceremonial grounds. Thus, the problem that Jesus addresses once more in this passage is the problem of the fragmented heart. Speaking in a patriarchically-dominated society, he attempts to protect the dignity of women by claiming that divorce is not to be permitted except for the cause of unchastity. However, if Jesus' polemical remark is taken out of context and the specific concern with the problem of ceremonial uncleanliness is ignored, the remark itself is not broad enough to cover all the problems of divorce that confront a contemporary society. It is therefore essential to remember that its chief function is not to provide an exhaustive teaching on divorce, but to return his audience to the problem of the heart.

A second step with respect to this problem can be taken if we turn to a parallel passage in the tenth chapter of Mark, verses eleven and twelve, where we find these words:

> And He said to them, "Whoever divorces his wife and marries another woman commits adultery against her; and if she herself divorces her husband and marries another man, she is committing adultery (Mk 10.11,12).

In interpreting this passage, everything hinges upon how we translate the Greek word *kai* in the second and third clauses. Though it is usually translated "and," it may also be rendered "in order to"; and if that is done in this case, the significance of the passage is transformed immediately. Let us then translate the verses in Mark with this possibility in mind:

> And He said to them, "Whoever divorces his wife *in order to* marry another woman, commits adultery against her; and if she divorces her husband *in order to* marry another man, she is committing adultery."

In the light of this passage, let us now return to the person who places the blindfold on his head in order to deal with the problem of adultery. Jesus has already suggested that if the blindfold slips and the person glances at a woman to lust after her, he has already committed adultery with her in his heart. However, now he suggests that if this same individual uses a ceremonial excuse to divorce his wife *in order to* marry another woman, who might perhaps be the one he has glimpsed out of the corner of his eye, he is to be condemned and to be called back to the sanctity of his own most intimately personal relationship. The phrase in Mark points to the possibility of a marriage triangle involving a man, his wife, and another woman, and indeed, in the Gentile context to which Mark was addressing himself, it even suggests the possibility of a glance in which the lust of the wife is also brought under judgment. As Mark says, "and if she divorces her husband *in order to* marry another man, she is committing adultery."

If we return to the original passage in Matthew, we do not find the problem of the marriage triangle made explicit, for Matthew is addressing a Jewish audience and is concerned primarily with the rabbinical dispute about the problem of divorce. By contrast, Mark who has a Gentile audience in mind does not address this dispute and hence does not include the phrase, "except for the cause of unchastity." However, when we take these two passages together and relate them to Jesus' earlier attack upon those who fail to confront their own lustful hearts, a richer teaching emerges. Moreover, when we examine the original passage in Matthew more closely, we find another important consideration that ought to be made explicit. In Matthew Jesus says, "I say to you that everyone who divorces his wife, except for the cause of unchastity, makes her commit adultery;

and whoever marries a divorced woman commits adultery." In the original text, the verb in the phrase "makes her commit adultery" is in the passive voice, and as a result, the implication is that divorce on ceremonial grounds to marry another woman makes the wife *a recipient of the adultery of her husband*. Thus, in Mark we find the marriage triangle moving in two directions, while in the Hebrew context the discussion of divorce focuses on the problem of uncleanness. However, even here, if divorce occurs for merely ceremonial reasons, the man is blamed, not only for the lust of his own heart, but also for inflicting the problem on his wife.

When Jesus says that whoever marries a divorced woman commits adultery, the polemical target of his remarks is not the woman but the man who has availed himself of a rabbinical excuse for divorcing his wife on ceremonial grounds. Thus, Jesus says that such a man is not only forbidden to divorce his wife except for the cause of adultery, but is also forbidden to marry another woman who has been made available by the original lustfulness of the Pharisaical system. Jesus' teaching about divorce should not be erected into a universal law, for what he has to say about it is addressed to the fragmentation that lies at the foundation of the pharisaical mentality. It would therefore be a radical mistake to interpret the very passages that are addressed to the Pharisees from a pharisaical point of view.

Perhaps the best way to express the flexibility of the New Testament teaching about the problem before us is to recall the remarks of Paul about this same issue in the seventh chapter of I Corinthians. In verses ten through sixteen of that chapter Paul says:

> But to the married I give instructions, not I, but the Lord, that the wife should not leave her husband (but if she does leave, let her remain unmarried, or else be reconciled with her husband), and that the husband should not send his wife away. But to the rest I say, not the Lord, that if any brother has a wife who is an unbeliever, and she consents to live with him, let him not send her away. And a woman who has an unbelieving husband, and he consents to live with her, let her not send her husband away. For the unbelieving husband is sanctified through his wife, and the unbelieving wife is sanctified through her believing husband; for otherwise your children are unclean, but now they are holy. Yet if the unbelieving one leaves, let him leave; the brother or the sister

is not under bondage in such cases, but God has called us to peace. For how do you know, O wife, whether you will save your husband? Or how do you know, O husband, whether you will save your wife? (1 Cor 7.10–16).

In considering this passage, it is important to notice that Paul is confronting a Gentile community and that as a result, the church is faced with the problem of "mixed" marriages for the first time. Thus, Paul re-interprets the original teaching of Jesus to address the new situation, remaining true to its spirit, but altering the letter of the law appropriately. Thus Paul says, if both partners in the marriage are believers, they should stay married; if one is a believer and the other is not, they should attempt to remain together if both consent; but if the one who is an unbeliever departs, he or she should be allowed to go, dissolving the marriage relation in a Gentile context where the distinction between believer and unbeliever comes to focus.

However, there is something deeper that must also be said about the problem of marriage which can be addressed to every situation and which captures the spirit with which both Jesus and Paul attempted to deal with the issue. The pressures upon marriage arise from three places: some come from the outside; some come from within; and others come from the vertical context of our relationship with God. Yet corresponding to the three places where the problem of marriage must be confronted are three questions which echo in the teaching of Jesus. First, "What have we been forgiven?" Second, "What are we asked to forgive?" And in the third place, "What forgiveness are we asked to accept?" The first of these questions points toward our relationship with God and grounds the entire discussion. The second points to our relationship with others and gives our discussion a horizontal thrust. And the third points within, asking us to come to terms with our fragmented hearts. These questions, which reflect the most crucial dimensions of the Sermon on the Mount, take us further than any others because they are relevant to *every* situation. But especially with respect to marriage, the questions, "What have we been forgiven?" "What are we asked to forgive?" and "What forgiveness do we accept?" serve to place us at the center of the gospel.

CHAPTER IX

THE PROBLEM OF FALSE VOWS

❦

In the fifth chapter of Matthew, Jesus deals with five practical problems about which he wishes to instruct his disciples. The first is the problem of murder and anger; the second, the problem of adultery and divorce; the third, the problem involved in making false vows; the fourth, the problem of retaliation; and the fifth, the problem of loving one's enemies. Having dealt with the first two problems already, we turn now to the third, which Jesus addresses in the following way in verses thirty-three through thirty-seven:

> Again you have heard that the ancients were told, "You shall not make false vows, but shall fulfill your vows to the Lord." But I say to you, make no oath at all, either by heaven, for it is the throne of God, or by the earth, for it is the footstool of His feet, or by Jerusalem, for it is the city of the great King. Nor shall you make an oath by your head, for you cannot make one hair white or black. But let your statement be, "Yes, yes" or "No, no"; and anything beyond these is of evil (Mt 5.33–37).

In discussing this passage, it is important to remember the phrase with which it is bracketed, for it is this phrase that establishes the framework for each of the problems Jesus considers in this chapter. That phrase, of course, is the claim, "You have heard that it has been said . . . , but I say unto you. . . ." When Jesus makes this claim, he is pointing not only to the past out of which his disciples had emerged, but also toward the new world into which he wishes to lead them. Moreover, when he says "I say unto you," he speaks with an authority that comes from God; he speaks directly to the core of human existence; and he points to concrete contexts of interaction where interpersonal relationships are central. Thus, the phrase with which Jesus begins his teaching in this passage points backward to the past; it points forward to a new world; it points upward to words that come from God; it points downward to the center of our being; and it points outward to the social context into which Jesus calls his followers.

It is impossible to read the Sermon on the Mount without attending to the past, and we must always bring the passage under discussion into relation with its Old Testament context. However, when Jesus says, "You have heard that it has been said . . . , but I say unto you . . . ," the backward thrust of his message is balanced by a counterthrust into a new and richer world where Jesus himself intends to establish God's kingdom. The content of Jesus' utterances also call our attention to the fact that God stands in the background of the discussion and is the ultimate foundation in terms of which the entire discussion is meaningful. We cannot read the discussion of the practical problems Jesus considers in any light other than the light that comes from God. Therefore, the backward and the forward thrust of the message must be placed within the context of the overarching presence of God, and God himself is the ground upon which the entire discussion stands rooted. Yet because his words are rooted there, Jesus is also able to speak directly to the heart, for the core of our being is the place where we come into contact with God as the ground of our existence. As St. Augustine insisted so forcefully, the intersection of eternity and time is to be found at the center of the human soul.[1] When the backward, forward, upward, and downward dimensions of the message are finally brought together, Jesus also calls our attention to the social relevance of his teaching and brings us face to face with practical problems of interpersonal interaction that must be confronted. The Sermon on the Mount is sometimes read as though it has nothing to do with the past and is something radically new; it is sometimes read as though it were a social gospel, and as though it had nothing to do with the God that grounds it; and it is sometimes read as though it is socially irrelevant and has to do *only* with God, where its interpersonal dimension merely points to an ideal kingdom that will one day come, but which has very little bearing upon our current situation. All three of these misreadings reflect a failure to sort out the five strands upon which the Sermon depends and to come to terms with the past, the future, the divine, the human, and the social dimensions the message reflects.

In turning to the passage before us in the light of these five dimensions, the first issue to be faced about verse thirty-three is the question, "What is the Old Testament context that lies behind the discussion?" The problem of making false vows arises from the Old Testament tradition, and there are three places in the first five books of the Bible where this issue is discussed. The first is Leviticus 19:12: "And you shall not swear falsely by My name, so as to profane the name of your God; I am the Lord." The second significant passage is to be found in the thirtieth chapter of Numbers, verse two:

> If a man makes a vow to the Lord, or takes an oath to bind himself with a binding obligation, he shall not violate his word; he shall do according to all that proceeds out of his mouth (Nm 30.2).

Finally, in the twenty-third chapter of Deuteronomy, verses twenty-one through twenty-three, we find these words:

> When you make a vow to the Lord your God, you shall not delay to pay it, for it would be sin in you, and the Lord your God will surely require it of you. However, if you refrain from vowing, it would not be sin in you. You shall be careful to perform what goes out of your [mouth], just as you have voluntarily vowed to the Lord your God, what you have promised (Dt 23.21–23).

Jesus' initial reference to the problem of false vows in verse thirty-three no doubt has these Old Testament passages in mind.

What is the purpose of taking a vow, and why does Jesus, and indeed, the Old Testament tradition, dwell on the problem? The point of oath-taking is twofold. In the first place, to take an oath is to give an external sign that is binding upon the heart. One has an intention, makes an utterance, and takes an oath in order to link the intention and the utterance with the public context in which that intention or utterance is expressed. The intention or the utterance is brought into relation with a social framework by taking an oath, and the oath itself serves as a cord to bind the private and the public realms together. For example, it is not by accident that oaths are taken in a courtroom where what is at stake is an issue that has to do with the social fabric of society. Oaths of this kind imply that the private intentions and private utterances that might otherwise be made are bound to the social fabric of the society in which they occur, and the taking of an oath in a courtroom is a way of sealing this fact.

Oath-taking was also performed in the Hebrew tradition in order to certify the truthfulness of one's own words by appealing to an authority higher than one's self. One has something to say and says it, but then adds: "I want to bind myself by mentioning an authority higher than myself in whose name my utterance is to be construed. So I take an oath unto the Lord in order to appeal to a higher authority in order to provide certification that what I say is true."

When Jesus deals with the problem of oath-taking, he not only returns to the Old Testament tradition but also has a contemporary rabbinical dispute in mind, and it is this rabbinical dispute to which he responds with his own revolutionary teaching. The dispute arises with reference to Deuteronomy 23:21–23, where the Lawgiver says:

> When you make a vow to the Lord your God, you shall not delay
> to pay it, for it would be sin in you . . . . However, if you refrain
> from vowing, it would not be sin in you (Dt 23.21–23).

The rabbinical question with respect to this passage can be formulated simply: "What does the phrase 'refrain from vowing' mean?" On the surface, the passage seems to refer to a person's failing to make a vow and hence, refraining from it. But perhaps the passage might be interpreted in the following way: If we refrain from vowing to the Lord, but vow with reference to some other content, it would not be sinful for us to break our word, since we would then be bound by that other content and not by God. Now it is at this point that the rabbinical dispute begins. The strict construction of the passage suggests that what is under discussion is simply oath-taking as such, where one is bound if he takes it, and not bound if he refrains from doing so. However, the more liberal construction suggests that so long as one refrains from vowing *to the Lord,* it would not be sinful for him to break his vow, since it was made upon something *less binding than God.* Many of the Pharisees whom Jesus opposed preferred the more liberal interpretation, claiming that if one takes a vow to the Lord, he is bound, and if he vows upon the Temple, he is bound, while if he vows upon the altar of the Temple, he is not. In fact, an intricate framework for oath-taking was in place at the time Jesus spoke, and the intricacies of maneuvering one's way through it in the course of social interchange invoked the casuistry that lay behind the pharisaical degenerations of rabbinical disputes.[2]

Lest we think this problem has nothing to do with us, let me call your attention to some interchanges in ordinary English that make it clear that the problem we are considering has a bearing on our own situation. We have all been in situations where someone said that he would do something, and when the time came to fulfill the bargain replied, "But I did not say I promised." Or what about the occasions when a child makes a promise and later on reveals triumphantly that he had crossed his fingers? Or what about those occasions when children are asked to honor their commitments and say, "But I did not say 'Cross my heart and hope to die' "? What are children attempting to do when they speak in this way? They are trying to escape the implications of their commitments and are also suggesting that oaths are not binding unless they come from the core of one's existence, designated by the heart, on the one hand, and by one's own life and death on the other.

But if these illustrations serve to shift our attention from an archaic context into the present, what does Jesus have to say about the issue? He makes his own positive assertion in verses thirty-four through thirty-six when he claims, "But I say to you, make no oath at all, either by heaven, or by the earth, or by Jerusalem, or by your own head." Moses had been very careful to enumerate the kinds of oath that could be taken, for oath-taking was a crucial dimension of the social fabric of the community he was attempting to establish. However, in the light of the rabbinical dispute about the issue and the pharisaical degeneration with respect to the problem, Jesus attempts to fulfill the original intention of the Law by claiming: "Do not make any oaths at all; and in addition, do not certify the truthfulness of your assertions by swearing either upon heaven, earth, Jerusalem, or your own head."

Notice especially the descending order of the words Jesus uses here and their spiritual relevance to an attempt to escape the consequences of one's vows by appealing to something lower than God himself. Jesus says, "Do not swear upon heaven instead of God because heaven is God's throne; do not swear upon the earth, which appears to be less binding, because the earth is God's footstool; do not swear by Jerusalem, which is less binding still, for that is the city where the King sits; and do not swear upon your own head, making yourself the ground of your own utterance, for you are unable to make the hair on your head either white or black." Of course, in the strict sense we can alter the color of our hair. But in this context Jesus is talking about the aging process which points to our own finiteness and, therefore, suggests that it can be certified only if it points to God who grounds heaven, earth, Jerusalem, and our own finite condition.

The core of Jesus' constructive suggestion about how to deal with the problem of oath-taking is to be found in verse thirty-seven where he advises us to certify the truth of our assertions by saying simply, "Yes, yes; no, no." But why does he ask us to speak so directly? The problem of the Sermon on the Mount is the problem of God and the soul and the problem of the vertical relation in which we stand to him. And we stand in that relation by responding from the center of our existence with either a "yes" or a "no." In the passage before us, we have a discussion of oath-taking that begins with the past, moves through a rabbinical dispute, presupposes a religious degeneration, and drives toward a new world by saying, "Do not take oaths at all." Jesus then warns us not to take an oath by something less than God in order to excuse ourselves from obligations, for everything less than God is what it is because it is related to him. The heavens are his throne, the earth is his footstool, the city of Jerusalem is the place where the King he has appointed sits, and the color of our hair is what is is only because it is grounded in him. Finally, if that framework is presupposed, we can then proceed to quit taking oaths altogether and to say simply "yes" or "no." For the "yes" on the one hand, and the "no" on the other, serves as the cord that binds us to the sustaining ground of our existence.

But the question still remains, "How do we begin to establish the social framework that is implicated in Jesus' suggestion?" It is very tempting to interpret Jesus' remarks to imply that we should *never* take an oath; and, as a result, a provision has been made in the courtroom for us to make an affirmation rather than to take a civil oath. As a result, the simple affirmation, "Yes, yes," replaces the solemn oath "so help me God." However, if we become preoccupied with the absolute injunction against taking an oath, we will miss the significance of Jesus' teaching entirely. In fact, it is possible to be pharisaical about *not* taking oaths, especially if the refusal to do so reflects a wish to be true to the letter of the Scripture. By contrast, Jesus is simply asking us to say "yes" or "no," and in meaning it, to stand in direct correlation with him. Thus, in a pharisaical context he tells us to repudiate oath-taking altogether, and to replace the labyrinthine framework that allows us to repudiate our obligations with straightforward communication.

If one is asked to take an oath in a formal context, he should feel perfectly free to do so, for what Jesus is discussing here is the necessity for a simple affirmation or denial that binds us directly to him. It is essential that we not focus on the text myopically, regenerating the very problem Jesus was attempting to address. Religious leaders are often masters at this, and we can easily become masters as well, especially since the words in question here are words from Jesus himself. The hermeneutical lesson to be learned in this case is that we must not simply focus our attention upon the surface of the text, but must attempt to understand its significance within the larger context of which it is a part. The point is to get to the crux of the matter, and in this case what is crucial has to do with the relation in which we stand to God.

Jesus' radical teaching about oath-taking inverts the structure of the pharisaical tradition, suggesting that a simple affirmation or denial, uttered in direct correlation with God, makes it unnecessary to introduce another context to ground the truth of our assertions. The authenticity of the "yes" and the "no," emphasized by repetition— "Yes, yes," "No, no"—points to this grounding relation, and if that grounding relation is in place, the hierarchy of mediators can be laid aside. "Do not swear," Jesus says, "upon heaven, or earth, or Jerusalem, or upon your own head, for all these things stand in direct correlation with God." That relation is the ground of every other relation, and therefore, the social implications of discourse will take care of themselves when they are rooted in that framework. The first question to ask about the problem before us pertains to the Old Testament context, the second question focuses upon the rabbinical dispute that arises from it, the third asks about the religious tendency to make a degenerate response to the problem, the fourth concerns Jesus' attempt to bring the discussion back to God and the soul, and the fifth asks about the relation between this attempt and the larger social situation. By considering all these issues, the problem of false oaths is finally resolved by an injunction to truthful and straightforward communication.

One of the most interesting facts about the psychology of oath-taking is that the more they are multiplied, the less likely they are to be fulfilled. If I must appeal to an authority other than myself to ground my own truthfulness, there is an external relation between me and the truth, where the distance in question is just as great as the distance between my own finiteness and the authority to which I appeal. Moreover, the greater the distance, the more room I have to slither away from my social obligations. Perhaps what grounds my commitment are the heavens; perhaps it is the earth; perhaps Jerusalem; or perhaps the color of my hair as a reflection of my own finitude. In all these cases, there is an external relation between the utterance and its ground, and Jesus attempts to move beyond this externality by asking us to restrict ourselves to a simple "yes" or "no." In this case, the core of our being is invoked; in this case, we are brought into direct correlation with God; in this case, externality vanishes; and when this occurs, our utterance can be trusted. Thus Jesus moves beyond the pharisaical mentality and the self-justification that often characterizes it, pointing instead to a divine simplicity.

Finally, Jesus says that anything transcending this divine simplicity ultimately derives from evil, or perhaps more accurately, from the evil one. Why does he say this? He does so because anything more than a simple affirmation or denial entangles us in a net of legalistic complexity, and a net of this kind is often a reflection of negative intentions. The spider's web through which the Pharisee attempts to weave his way in his dealings with others turns him away from the one thing needed, and this one thing is a direct relation with God that transcends the degeneration of ritualistic behavior. We are brought back, then, to the crucial summary point of the Law and the Prophets that Jesus gives us in the twenty-second chapter of Matthew: "Love God with all your heart, your soul, and strength; and love your neighbor as yourself" (Mt 22.37–39). When these two things are done, the spider's web in which we will otherwise become enmeshed will be less binding, and in some cases, it will vanish altogether.

CHAPTER X

THE PROBLEM OF RETALIATION

❦

In this chapter we turn to verses thirty-eight through forty-two of the fifth chapter of Matthew where Jesus deals with the fourth practical problem he addresses in the Sermon on the Mount. The problem under discussion is the problem of revenge, or perhaps better, the problem of retaliation; and he formulates it in his customary fashion in verses thirty-eight and thirty-nine of Chapter Five:

> You have heard that it was said, "An eye for an eye, and a tooth for a tooth." But I say to you, do not resist him who is evil (Mt 5.38,39).

These are perhaps the hardest words Jesus has spoken to his disciples, for they are not only difficult to understand, but harder still to live by. These words are easily transformed into mere metaphors that have no relation to the real world; they have sometimes become the excuse for weakness and cowardice; they have become a mask that hides a slave mentality; and they have been construed as the ground for indecisiveness, not only in interpersonal relations, but also in the larger context of social and political interaction. This passage therefore calls for careful interpretation, and for an intelligent and conscientious response from those to whom it is addressed.

The first step in understanding the problems Jesus discusses in Chapter Five is to trace them back to their Old Testament origins. In this case, there are three passages that have a bearing on the problem before us. The first is to be found in the twenty-first chapter of Exodus, verses twenty-two through twenty-four:

> And if men struggle with each other and strike a woman with child so that she has a miscarriage, yet there is no further injury, he shall surely be fined as the woman's husband may demand of him; and he shall pay as the judges decide. But if there is any further injury, then you shall appoint as a penalty life for life, eye for eye, tooth for tooth, hand for hand, foot for foot (Ex 21.22–24).

The second passage relevant to the issue at hand is to be found in Leviticus 24:17–20:

> And if a man takes the life of any human being, he shall surely be put to death. And the one who takes the life of an animal shall make it good, life for life. And if a man injures his neighbor, just as he has done, so it shall be done to him: fracture for fracture, eye for eye, tooth for tooth; just as he has injured a man, so it shall be inflicted on him (Lv 24.17–20).

Finally, the third passage to be considered occurs in Deuteronomy 19:15–21:

> A single witness shall not rise up against a man on account of any iniquity or any sin which he has committed; on the evidence of two or three witnesses a matter shall be confirmed. If a malicious witness rises up against a man to accuse him of wrongdoing, then both the men who have the dispute shall stand before the Lord, before the priests and the judges who will be in office in those days. And the judges shall investigate thoroughly; and if the witness is a false witness and he has accused his brother falsely, then you shall do to him just as he had intended to do to his brother. Thus you shall purge the evil from among you. And the rest will hear and be afraid, and will never again do such an evil thing among you. Thus you shall not show pity; life for life, eye for eye, tooth for tooth, hand for hand, foot for foot (Dt 19.15–21).

In attempting to understand these passages, it is important to remember that they are addressed to an emerging nation that had been enslaved for more than four hundred years, and that within this context, any act of aggression had always been repaid with an even more violent response. These former slaves who had been subjected to extreme violence for the slightest act of insubordination were thus inclined to imitate their masters, and as a result, they tended to respond to aggressiveness with a form of aggression that outstripped the original injury. Thus, the purpose of these Mosaic passages was to circumscribe the retaliatory response so that it was exactly appropriate to the injury inflected, and to take the first step in the transition from a violent, lawless society to a society in which law emerges and where justice and equality are related. When a contemporary reader encounters these passages, he no doubt reacts to their violence; but when a former slave is confronted with these same pronouncements, he is liberated from the slavery from which he has come into the first stage of the development of a civilized society.[1]

The passages before us suggest that the justice being called for is based on strict equality, so that when one cuts off the hand of his neighbor, he does not sacrifice his life, but only a hand. In addition, these passages *serve to place these rules of equality within a juridical context*. Thus we find that witnesses, judges, and the larger juridical framework are always invoked as the context in which disputes of this kind are to be adjudicated. The point of the Mosaic law in these cases is therefore to move the act of aggression and the act of retaliation from the wilderness into the center of a civilized society, so that problems of this kind can be dealt with rationally as the law requires.

When Jesus delivers the Sermon on the Mount, he confronts a quite different situation. The Jews have been liberated from slavery, the Law has been established, and the nation has made the transition from savagery to the orderly structure of a genuine community. However, the Hebrew people are also confronted by the weight of Roman oppression, and the Romans express this oppression by refusing to submit to the legal system the Jews had been so careful to develop. The problem with which Jesus is confronted, then, is this: "What shall I say in this new context of oppression, where oppression itself is to be dealt with against the background of the Law?" There are only two responses: return to the slave mentality of Egypt and the savagery that accompanied it, or move forward to a creative response that transcends the original requirements of the Law. Jesus chooses this second alternative, formulating his response in accord with it in verses thirty-eight through forty-two:

> You have heard that it was said, "An eye for an eye, and a tooth for a tooth." But I say to you, do not resist him who is evil; but whoever slaps you on your right cheek, turn to him the other also. And if anyone wants to sue you, and take your shirt, let him have your coat also. And whoever shall force you to go one mile, go with him two. Give to him who asks of you, and do not turn away from him who wants to borrow from you (Mt 5.38–42).

Let us consider first the slap in the face. Perhaps a Roman general comes to Jerusalem, and as he works his way down the Palestinian streets, he slaps a person who stands in his way. The slap in question is clearly an insult, for the text is very careful to assert that it is the *right* cheek that is slapped, which implies that the blow is delivered with the back of one's hand. This episode also involves a nonjudicial situation and implies the kind of social inequality that would have made a legal remedy impossible. It is useless for a person who has been slapped by a Roman general to appeal to the Mosaic law, and as a result, the only alternative responses appear to be spontaneous retaliation or abject submission. However, in the passage before us Jesus says that there is a better way, and that this better way is to turn the other cheek. It is important to notice that Jesus does not say, "Having been slapped in the face, be slapped a second time as well." Rather, he says, "After you have been slapped on the right cheek, *turn the other also*." An act of the kind Jesus recommends is deliberate, and it involves a transition from passivity to positive action. The slap has been delivered; one turns the other cheek; but the transition involved in doing so can presumably be effected *in an almost regal fashion*. Moreover, when one turns the other cheek with human dignity, the possibility exists for a breakdown, or perhaps, a breakthrough into the consciousness of the one who delivers the blow, driving the transaction to a higher level.[2]

Let us turn now to the second case Jesus considers. This time his remarks do not refer to a superior who slaps a person who has no legal recourse, but to a person on the same social level with another who wishes to bring a suit against him for the shirt on his back. Perhaps such a person has not fully appreciated the oppressive predicament he shares with his neighbor, and as a way of repressing his awareness of it, turns toward him to take his shirt away. But even if this should prove to be the case, what does Jesus say? He suggests that we respond, not by appealing to a legal context, but by giving our coat away as well. In doing so, our neighbor who shares our predicament might be turned away from an abstract system of justice to the larger problem of oppression, and might be forced to deal with it by moving to a higher level of responsiveness.

The third example Jesus considers in this passage is even clearer. In this case, he presupposes a military context explicitly, mentioning the familiar example of a soldier who compels us to carry his baggage for a mile. Jesus tells us that in such a case, we should not only go one mile, but two; for what is merely servile in the first mile *becomes mastery in the second*. The first slap of insult, the passivity of the law court, and the servility displayed under the heavy load for the first mile become victories when one turns the other cheek, when one gives his coat away, and when one chooses to travel the second mile. The long journey from slavery to law to the oppression that seeks to override it finally points to a higher level of human behavior, and Jesus asks us to embrace it by turning the other cheek, by giving our coat away, and by walking the second mile.

In this connection, we should perhaps remember the occasion when Jesus was carrying his cross through the streets of Jerusalem and when the Roman guard in charge of his execution demanded that Simon of Cyrene get down under the cross and carry his load for a mile (Mt 27.32). Simon reacts initially to the soldier's demand just as we would, refusing to obey. However, a transformation occurs when he finally bends down, looks in Jesus' face, and begins to carry the cross; for when he does, the oppressed man who was forced to walk one mile becomes a victorious man who is able to walk two. Jesus' remarks in this passage are intended to suggest that there are only a few alternatives available for life in society. One is the alternative of savagery; another is the alternative of law; the third is the alternative of the oppressive power that outstrips the law; while the fourth is a way of living that might appear to be servile in the beginning, but that issues in absolute mastery in the end. The question Jesus poses is whether in extreme situations there is a way of responding that leads beyond retaliation to a higher way of living, and his reply in this passage is that there is.

If we choose to move in this direction, some problems inevitably remain, the first of which is that having turned the other cheek, we might wonder if we have the right to turn our children's cheeks as well. I assume that Jesus' answer to this question is "no," for he speaks in this passage in the first person singular, implying that the only person who can act on his advice is the one being addressed.[3] The reason for this is that what is in question in acting in the way Jesus demands is the center of our existence in correlation with God, and *no one can stand in that place for another.* Sometimes one's children also choose to stand there, and when that choice is made, a new kind of community is generated where each member can preserve his own integrity. However, it is not our task to ask another person to turn the other cheek, but to respond for ourselves to the injunctions of Jesus formulated here.

Of course, we must admit that acting on Jesus' demands will not succeed with beasts, for the time has not yet come when the lions will lie down with the lambs, and when all the spears will be beaten into pruning hooks (Is 11.6,7). Moreover, it is unlikely that Jesus' injunctions are intended to apply to the larger contexts of societies and nations, for the new community he envisages can only be actualized piecemeal, a step at a time, here and now. In this passage, Jesus is addressing particular situations, and he is asking us to respond to them in individual terms.

There is one final verse that serves to bring Jesus' discussion of the problem before us to a conclusion, but which also shifts the scene in a more redemptive direction. In verse forty-two, the person who has been slapped, the person who has given away his coat, and the person who has walked the second mile is able to stand erect. In verse forty-one Jesus says, "Whoever shall force you to go one mile go with him two," but in verse forty-two he adds, "Give to him who asks of you, and do not turn away from him who wants to borrow from you." What has happened in between those two verses to the one who has been slapped, who has given his coat away, and who has walked the second mile? He has been transformed from a slave who can be oppressed into a human being from whom someone else can make a request.[4] In this verse, Jesus does not say, "Give whatever you are asked to give," but he does say "Give." And he does not say, "Lend whatever you are asked to lend," but he does say "Do not turn away."[5] Yet the most important point to notice is that both these acts are made possible by the fact that the person being addressed has finally been able to stand erect, having endured the stages of development to which the slap, the cloak, and the second mile call our attention.

When I was a child, one of the episodes I remember best was the day I met the man who founded the Kraft Cheese Company. He had invited my father to preach in his church in Chicago, and when we arrived, he took us out to the North Shore where we spent the weekend in one of the most beautiful houses I have ever seen. On Monday morning before we returned, Mr. Kraft asked us to come to his office, and as he and my father talked, he suddenly picked up a handful of caramels from his desk and put them in my hand, responding to an unspoken request. On the way to the airport, I offered the chauffeur a piece of candy which he refused, but when I told him that Mr. Kraft had given them to me, he said laughingly, "In that case, I'll take one."

It was not until several years later that I realized that the irony of his response might not have been merely ironical. On this second occasion, my parents and I visited Mr. Kraft in his summer home, and on Sunday night before he returned to work in Chicago he spent an hour and a half cutting flowers in his garden. Later, my father asked the chauffeur, who was loading the flowers in the car, what he was going to do with them. He replied, "Every Monday night we take flowers to a hospital, and Mr. Kraft walks up and down the halls giving them away." When I heard that story, I not only saw our host in a different light, but I finally understood the non-ironical dimension of the chauffeur's response several years earlier, "In that case, I'll take one."

J. L. Kraft started his business by pushing a cart in Chicago when he had only one roll of cheese to sell; he did not have any employees; he did not have a chauffeur; and he did not have a beautiful house. Over the years, he of course became very successful, but my recollection of him has to do with the caramels he gave a child, with the fact that he had a chauffeur who was willing to take one when he heard they came from him, and with the story I heard about what he did with the flowers every Monday night. How many second miles did the old man walk before he became president of the Kraft Cheese Company? How many coats did he give away? And how many times was he slapped in the face? More than once, I suspect, but I also know that having come to stand at the top of a skyscraper, he was able to give. It is the kind of life that both stands erect and gives something away that Jesus asks his followers to embrace.

CHAPTER XI

LOVE YOUR ENEMIES

❦

In this chapter we turn to the fifth practical problem Jesus discusses with his disciples in the fifth chapter of Matthew. He has spoken already about murder and anger, about adultery and divorce, about the problem of false oaths, and about the problem of retaliation, and in verses forty-three through forty-eight of Chapter Five, he concludes this part of his Sermon by focusing on the issue that brings all the others to concrete focus. In these five verses he tells his followers to love their enemies, and in doing so, he asks them to embrace the same kind of perfection that God himself has already expressed toward the world.

Jesus formulates the problem before us in verse forty-three of Chapter Five when he claims: "You have heard that it was said, 'You shall love your neighbor, and hate your enemy.' " As in previous cases, he thereby returns us to the Old Testament context in which the command to love our neighbors as ourselves was first expressed. In the nineteenth chapter of Leviticus, verse eighteen, the Lawgiver says: "You shall not take vengeance, nor bear any grudge against the sons of your people, but you shall love your neighbor as yourself; I am the Lord." These remarks were addressed originally to the Jews, and they have as their primary focus the relation between an individual Jew and his neighbor, commanding each of them to love his neighbor as himself. However, it is also important to notice that this injunction concludes with the phrase, "I am the Lord." The demand that we love

our neighbors as ourselves is an utterance made within the light that
comes from God, and as a result, the injunction is not only of ethical
significance, but also points to a spiritual bond between an individual
and his neighbor as they are both related to the sustaining ground of
their existence. The demand to love our neighbors as ourselves is
sustained by the God who makes it, and without that undergirding
ground, the demand itself would collapse into an unreachable ideal.

We should also notice that corresponding to this Old Testament
injunction is a rabbinical dispute, and in this case, the dispute is
formulated in the New Testament in the familiar question, "Who,
then, is my neighbor?" (Lk 10.29). The Jews had heard the words,
"Love your neighbor as yourself," but as their social and cultural
context became more complex, they quite naturally wondered who
should be included within the range of this injunction. Some scholars
responded to this question in a straightforward fashion, and their way
of doing so accounts for the last clause of verse forty-three. In Leviticus, Moses had said, "Love your neighbor as yourself," and had not
added the second clause, "Hate your enemy." This second clause is a
Pharisaical emendation, and Jesus adds it in his own formulation to
reflect their solution to the problem about who should be regarded as
one's neighbor. If one's neighbor is only a friend, or a kinsman, or a
son of Israel in the strict sense of the term, it is natural to keep the
neighbor and the enemy distinct and to direct one's hatred toward his
enemies. Therefore, when Jesus says, "You have heard that it was
said," he first quotes Moses; then presupposes the rabbinical dispute
about who counts as a neighbor, knowing that some of the Pharisees
have decided already that neighbors are to be distinguished from
enemies; and therefore concludes verse forty-three with the non-
Mosaic phrase, "and hate your enemy."

But how does Jesus respond to the scholarly emendation of
Moses' original pronouncement? He does so in verses forty-four and
forty-five of Chapter Five by claiming: "But I say to you, love your
enemies, and pray for those who persecute you in order that you may
be sons of your Father who is in heaven." In another gospel, Jesus
responds more concretely to the rabbinical dispute about Moses'
intentions by telling the story of the Good Samaritan. The usual

interpretation of this story suggests that Jesus' own people are being asked to regard the Samaritans as their neighbors and not to restrict their friendship to the sons of Israel (Lk 10.30–37). And indeed, this is one of Jesus' intentions, as the passage before us from the Sermon on the Mount clearly suggests. Yet we must not forget that the Samaritan of the story also regarded the Jew as an enemy, responding nevertheless to a man in need without regard to his own inclinations. Grace is thus the hidden theme of the Good Samaritan story, and within this context, the injunction to love our enemies is formulated in a story about an enemy who has already revealed himself to be a friend. In the Good Samaritan story, we are not simply being asked to expand our neighborhood, but to notice that the enemy has already taken the initiative; and that the injunction to love our enemies is rooted in the grace of God. It should not be surprising, then, that St. Augustine allegorized this passage, and that he chose to interpret the Good Samaritan as an image of the grace of God expressed in Christ.[1]

Yet even if the story of the Good Samaritan is a forceful expression of the fact that the command to love our enemies is grounded in the grace of God, how are we to understand the significance of the command itself in general terms? At least one way to do so is to notice that it is formulated in the present tense, the active voice, and the imperative mood. In this case, Jesus is *commanding* that we love our enemies; in using the active voice, he is implying that if this occurs, *we ourselves must do it*; and in formulating his command in the present tense, he is implying that loving our enemies *only on particular or isolated occasions is not enough*. In Greek the present tense does not normally designate simply a particular episode, but refers instead to continuous action. Thus Jesus says, "Keep on loving your enemies in a sequence of acts that stretch out into an indefinite future."

When we shift our attention from the form of Jesus' command to its context, the most obvious question becomes, "What does Jesus mean by the kind of love he commands us to express?" *Agape* as it is used in this passage means simply to act gratuitously in the best interest of our enemies, however we might happen to feel; and it is only because love is understood in these terms that it can be commanded. It is fruitless to command affection; it is impossible to command friendship; but the one thing that can be commanded is that we respond with gratuitous, unmerited, and unsolicited favor toward our enemies. Jesus expects us to do this through an act of will, no matter what the affective state of our psyche might be. When acts of this kind occur, affection and friendship sometimes result, but the striking fact about the gospel is that these results are derivative upon an act of love that is indifferent to the value of its object.[2] We can explain what friendship means in sociological or psychological terms with little difficulty. However, we cannot explain the possibility of friendship in more fundamental terms unless it is rooted in a gratuitous act of love that expresses itself spontaneously and refuses to calculate the degree to which the one to whom it is given deserves to receive it. When an act of this kind is performed repeatedly over an extended period of time, and when it is directed not only toward our neighbors, but also toward our enemies, a new kind of community can result. This kind of community, which is potentially universal in its range of reference, can become a reflection of the grace that God himself has already expressed toward the world.

One way to emphasize the divine context within which Jesus speaks is to notice that having said "Love your enemies," he also says, "Pray for those who persecute you." What does praying have to do with loving our enemies, and why does a reference to it occur immediately after love has been commanded? If the kind of love under discussion is an act of will rather than an expression of affection or friendship, and if the love in question invokes an unmerited act of favor even toward one's enemies, the only way an act of this kind can be grounded is in terms of the vertical relation in which I stand to God. God himself has already responded to the world in the way Jesus is asking us to respond to our enemies, and the story of the Good Samaritan has already called our attention to the unsolicited favor that Christ has chosen to express to his followers. Therefore, it is quite appropriate that having said, "Love your enemies," Jesus adds, "Pray for those who persecute you," for that second phrase serves to put the relation between me and my enemies within the larger context of our relation to the grace of God. In Leviticus the

Lawgiver says, "Love your neighbor as yourself; I am the Lord," and the implication of his claim is that the entire injunction is meaningless apart from a reference to God. But having extended that earlier injunction to include our enemies, Jesus also demands that we pray for those who persecute us, implying that is is only within the vertical space defined by our relation to God that we can find the power to act on his command.

This way of interpreting Jesus' intentions is confirmed by the last phrase of verse forty-five where he tells us that we are to love our enemies and pray for those who persecute us "in order that we might be children of our Father." The point of obeying Jesus' commands is that doing so enables us to be imitators of God, reflecting in our relations with others what God himself has already accomplished at a more primordial level. Thus, the command of Jesus to love our enemies presupposes that God has already loved us, and the command that we pray for those who persecute us serves to bring our relation to them within the vertical context of what God himself has already done. Thus, the original utterance, "I am the Lord," that gave significance to the original Mosaic formulation of the Law finally becomes the utterance of grace that serves to extend the Mosaic demand outward toward the larger world.

If in commanding us to love our enemies Jesus is asking us to imitate God, how does he express the specific characteristic we are being asked to reflect? At the end of verse forty-five he does so symbolically by saying, "He causes His sun to rise on the evil and the good, and sends rain on the righteous and the unrighteous" (Mt 5.45b). Sun and rain were crucial in the agricultural economy of those to whom Jesus was speaking, and he addressed them in these terms partly for this reason. However, Jesus' fundamental intention was to call into question the typical Jewish presupposition that good things happen to good people and that evil only besets those who are evil themselves. By contrast, Jesus points to the grace of God that he asks us to imitate by loving our enemies, and he does so by telling us that God sends the sun both to the good and to the evil, and sends rain both to the righteous and the unrighteous. The love we are being asked to imitate must therefore derive from a point that transcends the distinction between good and evil, and Jesus tells us that it is just such a standpoint from which God himself has chosen to act.[3] Some of Jesus' contemporaries had said, "Love your neighbor and hate your enemy"; and in making this formulation, they were perfectly clear about the distinction between them. However, in claiming that we must imitate God and that God himself sends sun and rain to both the just and the unjust, Jesus implies that what is most important is not the distinction between good and evil, the neighbor and the enemy, but the act of grace that God has already expressed toward the world.

In verses forty-six and forty-seven of Chapter Five, Jesus emphasizes the fact that some of his audience had failed to grasp the fundamental point by comparing them unfavorably with the people they most despised. In this passage he asks:

> For if you love those who love you, what reward have you? Do not even the tax-gatherers do the same? And if you greet your brothers only, what do you do more than others? Do not even the Gentiles do the same? (Mt 5.46,47).

In these verses the implicit identification of Jew and Gentile is intended to infuriate his listeners, implying that their own question, "Who, then, is my neighbor?" is asked from a standpoint that robs them of their religious distinctiveness. The paradox of Jesus' remarks at this point is that they refocus our attention upon the fact that the superiority of his message consists in his willingness to make the grace of God universally accessible. It is indeed the case that, as Paul later said, there is no difference between Jew and Gentile (Rom 2.9–29), but the significance of this point is that it drives us back to the ground of love from which the command to love our enemies emerges.

Having commanded us to love our enemies, and having suggested that love of this kind is grounded in the grace of God, Jesus finally brings his discussion in Chapter Five to a conclusion by saying, "Therefore be perfect, as your Father in heaven is perfect" (Mt 5.48). The concept of perfection is Jesus' way of bringing all the strands of his earlier discussion into a unity, and he does this by telling us that unity of this kind is achieved by imitating the perfection of God. If Jesus has indeed spoken to our inward condition, if he has spoken to our outward relations, if he has spoken about the upward dimension of his message that brings us into the light that shines from beyond, if he has spoken about the past and the relation of his teaching to it, and if he has led us into a new world where inward, outward, upward, backward, and forward dimensions are all brought together, the only word that summarizes the teaching that points in all those directions at once is the word "perfection."

The Beatitudes tell us what it means to be blessed, and to be the recipients of divine inner happiness. The metaphors of salt and light presuppose this inward transformation and bring it into an explicit relation with the larger world. Jesus also tells us that he has not come to destroy the past, but to bring it to fulfillment, and he illustrates how he intends to do this with reference to five practical problems. Thus the phrase, "It has been said . . . , but I say unto you," echoes from verses twenty-one through forty-seven of Chapter Five. But what is the capstone of the entire discussion? He finally formulates it by telling us to love our enemies just as God does, and by saying that our imitation of God can be complete only when we become replicas of God's divine perfection. What is the most perfect thing God ever did? Reaching down to his enemies to make it possible for them to become his friends. What is the most unexpected thing perfection ever did? Emptying itself, and not insisting upon its own intrinsic value. And what is the richest perfection conceivable? It is the perfection that gives itself away. At the conclusion of the fifth chapter of Matthew, Jesus tells us to love our enemies, and in doing so, to imitate the divine perfection he has already expressed.

PART III

SIX EXPRESSIONS OF PERFECTION

CHAPTER XII

BEING SEEN AND BEING NOTICED:
SECRET ACTS OF CHARITY

At the conclusion of Chapter Five, Jesus asks his followers to be perfect just as their Father in heaven is perfect, and as we have discovered in the course of our earlier discussion, the word "perfection" points primarily to the concept of maturity. To be perfect is to be what we were meant to become; to be perfect is to be mature; to be perfect is to move beyond the initial stage of poverty and emptiness into the fullness of a new life that God himself makes accessible. Jesus describes the content of this new life, first in the Beatitudes where divine happiness is bestowed; then in the metaphors of salt and light where it is brought into relation with the larger world; and finally in his discussion of five practical problems, where the teaching of the past is brought to fulfillment in a teaching of his own. The problem of murder and anger, the problem of adultery and divorce, the problem of false vows, the problem of retaliation, and the problem of how to respond to our enemies represent five contexts through which we must pass if we are to grasp what Jesus means by the concept of divine perfection.

If Jesus asks his followers to be perfect at the end of Chapter Five, a question quite naturally arises about how and where this is to be done. In the sixth chapter of Matthew and in the first six verses of Chapter Seven, he answers this question, first by drawing a crucial distinction, then by pointing to six specific regions in which divine perfection is to be expressed, and finally by suggesting that in each of these contexts, radical degeneration is a permanent possibility. The distinction Jesus draws is between being seen and being noticed, and he warns us that we will never be mature if our actions are performed primarily to be noticed by others. Against the background of this general warning, he then tells us how perfection should be expressed in the contexts of giving, praying, and fasting, and says how it should be expressed in the choices we make about which master to serve, in the way we deal with the problem of anxiety, and in how we judge the behavior of others in contrast with the way we judge ourselves. Finally, he suggests that a failure to express perfection in any of these contexts will produce a radical degeneration that will obstruct the maturity into which he is attempting to lead us. For every context in which perfection can be expressed, there is a corresponding way of missing the target. As a result, Jesus not only illustrates the kind of perfection he wishes us to embrace in each case, but also calls our attention to the specific ways in which we might be inclined to fall away from it.[1]

We have referred already to the general problem that lies behind some of the particular degenerations we must consider. As Jesus expresses the point in verse one of Chapter Six: "Beware of practicing your righteousness before men to be noticed by them; otherwise you have no reward with your Father who is in heaven." In Chapter Five, Jesus has said that his followers are the light of the world, and this clearly presupposes that he intends for their good deeds to be seen by others. However, a crucial distinction exists between being seen and being noticed, and an equally important contrast obtains between actions that call men's attention to the righteousness of God and good deeds that are performed simply to glorify the agent. As we discovered in our earlier discussion, the light that shines in the world is derivative upon a light that has come down from above, and the purpose of the good deeds that our light illuminates is to allow the perfection of God to be revealed. A proper understanding of the first verse of Chapter Six depends upon grasping the distinction between being seen and being noticed. Our good deeds are to be seen in order to become a pathway that leads to God, while the deeds about which we are warned in this verse are performed simply to call attention to ourselves. In this case, the observer is not carried beyond the works to their ground but *stops there*; and indeed, he does so because the one who performs them intends for this to occur. When being seen is replaced by being noticed, the righteousness we practice becomes like "filthy rags," and the divine perfection Jesus wishes us to express degenerates into a perfection of our own making (Is 64.6).

There are two dimensions of our nature that serve to explain our tendency to transform being seen into being noticed and to substitute a righteousness of our own for the righteousness of God. One of these dimensions is our inevitable tendency to sin, while the other is our equally powerful tendency to perform good deeds. The second tendency often attempts to compensate for the first, causing us to vacillate between these two dimensions of our nature. Indeed, the natural consciousness can be characterized as an interplay between these two poles, and as the warfare of the soul with itself in making its choices between good and evil. As these choices are forced upon us, we easily become a divided consciousness, vacillating between our sins, on the one hand, and our good deeds on the other. As a result, the perfection Jesus asks us to express, and the wholeness he wants to make accessible to us, simply collapse into a cluster of fragments. But how does Jesus himself propose to deal with the problem of the fragmented soul? He does so by suggesting that our good deeds not be performed as expressions of our own goodness, as a way of compensating for our sins, and in order to be noticed by others, but that they be performed as an expression of the perfection of God. It is imperative that the cyclical pattern of natural existence be broken, but this can be done only by performing good deeds that are to be seen rather than noticed.

God provides a way of dealing with the sinful side of our nature, and his way of doing so is expressed in I John 1.9. In this passage, the Apostle says, "If we confess our sins, he is faithful and just to forgive us our sins, and to free us from all unrighteousness" (I Jn 1.9). The word "confess" simply means to admit what we have done, and it implies nothing about the need to express our guilt or to engage in acts of contrition. Indeed, the more we dwell on our sins beyond the act of confession in the minimal sense, the more we attempt to compensate for them with good deeds that express the other dimension of our nature. However, if we accept the fact that confession frees us from unrighteousness, we will be less inclined to practice our own righteousness before others in order to be noticed, laying claim instead to the righteousness of God we are asked to reflect. When our good deeds are freed from the burden of compensating for our sins, they can then become a window that will allow the perfection of God to become visible, and when the cyclical pattern of human existence is broken, we can locate the standpoint of divine perfection from which Jesus has asked us to act.

One of the clearest illustrations that this is so is to be found in the warning Jesus gives in Chapter Six, verse one. In this verse he tells us that if we practice our righteousness before others in order to be noticed, we will receive no reward from our Father in heaven. There are no doubt rewards of other kinds to be found in this way, but rewards from God are received only when our good deeds point away from themselves to their divine ground, giving the one who performs them access to eternity. Righteous deeds that are performed in order to be noticed are constricting and constricted; those same deeds that are performed only to be seen open us up to what lies beyond; and when being noticed is displaced by being seen, the rewards from God express themselves in divine perfection that becomes visible in the real order. In the six specific contexts to which we now turn our attention, it is therefore essential to notice the difference between a perfection of our own and acts that express the perfection of God.

The first of the six contexts where Jesus asks us to embrace divine perfection is to be found in the sixth chapter of Matthew, verses two through four. In these verses he says:

> When therefore you give alms, do not sound a trumpet before you, as the hypocrites do in the synagogues and in the streets, that they may be honored by men. Truly I say to you, they have their reward in full. But when you give alms, do not let your left hand know what your right hand is doing that your alms may be in secret; and your Father who sees in secret will repay you (Mt 6.2–4).

The phrase that is translated here "giving alms" is perhaps rendered more accurately, "performing acts of charity," but in each case, what the words suggest are situations in which one gives a gift to a person in need who is of a lower station than oneself. The original thought that lies behind the passage is that when we engage in acts of charity, where the act itself does not express an emotional attachment or an erotic desire, but simply a willingness to bestow a gift gratuitously, we should do so by imitating God rather than by blowing a trumpet in the streets to be noticed by men. The hypocrites against whom much of the Sermon on the Mount was formulated did not proceed in this way, but instead, had a trumpet sounded in the synagogue before they placed their gifts upon the altar. And they did this in order to be noticed by others who had come there to worship. But there is another kind of trumpet sounding that Jesus also has in mind in this passage, for the verses before us refer not only to trumpets in the synagogues, but also to trumpets in the streets. Water was very scarce in Palestine; and one of the good deeds that religious leaders would sometimes perform would be to have water skins brought into the market place, have a trumpet sounded in the streets, and then stand beside the water as the benefactor who dispensed it to all those who were thirsty.[2] In this passage Jesus reminds his disciples of two contexts in which acts of charity are performed, and he warns them that when they perform acts of this kind, they must not do so in this way. Otherwise, he suggests that they will receive only a finite reward.

There are two familiar passages in Scripture that stand in striking contrast to the examples of sounding trumpets mentioned in these verses. The first is to be found in the Old Testament, where the prophet Isaiah says:

Ho! Every one who thirsts,
   come to the waters;
And you who have no money
   come, buy and eat.
Come, buy wine and milk
Without money and without cost (Is 55.1).

In this passage, God reaches out his arms to a thirsty world inviting us all to drink freely, while in the Matthew passage the hypocrite stands with folded arms, offering a drink to the people of Jerusalem in order to be noticed by them. The second important passage that stands in contrast with the behavior of the hypocrites is to be found in the fourth chapter of John where we find Jesus' conversation with the woman at the well. At one juncture Jesus says:

> Everyone who drinks of this water shall thirst again; but whoever drinks of the water that I shall give him shall never thirst; but the water that I shall give him shall become in him a well of water springing up to eternal life (Jn 4.13,14).

Jesus suggests to his followers that in performing acts of charity, they must not imitate the degenerate version of generosity to be encountered in the synagogues and the streets, especially when such acts are to be measured against a standard that God himself provides.

How do we succeed in moving from these degenerate contexts to the divine perfection to which Jesus wishes to direct our attention? He tells us in verse three that we can do so when we perform acts of charity without letting our left hand know what our right hand is doing. On the surface, this seems to be an injunction to replace pharisaical ostentation with innocent ignorance, but a careful analysis of the passage suggests that this is not the case. There are various kinds of knowing, and in this case the left hand's act of knowing is an act of calculation. The right hand reaches into the robe to find the money, and the left hand reaches over to calculate what will in fact be given. Thus Jesus implies that acts of charity must not be acts of calculation, not only in the sense that they are designed to win approval, but also insofar as the act itself reflects a calculating heart.[3] God himself gives freely; the hypocrites give in order to be noticed; and Jesus asks his followers to imitate God instead of them by giving without calculation.

There is something more to be found in this passage, for in verse four Jesus tells us that when we perform acts of charity, it is important that they be performed in secret. Just as the earlier point about the left and the right hand might seem to be an injunction to ignorance, the corresponding claim about secrecy might seem to reflect a preoccupation with one's private world that Jesus does not intend. What is it to perform acts of love in secret? The secret place is the centered place, and the centered place is to be contrasted with the merely external dimension of human existence. From beginning to end, the Sermon on the Mount attempts to draw the distinction between the center and the periphery of human existence: the central problem to be confronted is not murder, but the anger of the soul; the crucial problem is not adultery and divorce, but the attitude of the lustful heart; and since this is so, when acts of charity are performed, the most important fact about them is not their external expression, but the centered self from which they spring. Where do acts of charity originate? Jesus tells us that if they are to be authentic, they must originate from the secret place. This secret place is not a secret to be defended, nor a secret that is utterly inaccessible, but is instead the centered place where God himself promises to be present.

Jesus expresses this final point in the second clause of verse four by telling us that if our acts of charity are performed in secret, and if they derive from the center of our being, God himself will reward us. In this case, the implication is that God who sees in secret, and hence from the center of our being, will reward us there. Some translations mistakenly say that God who sees in secret will "reward you openly." However, the word "openly" is not in the original text, and it is certainly appropriate that it is not. The point of Jesus' pronouncement is not that our reward will express itself externally, but that it will be found at the place from which our centered action springs. Furthermore, this final phrase implies that the reward in question is not simply a reward *from* God but a reward *with* God.[4] As a result, the reward itself is not the expression of a merely external relation with the ground of our existence, but a reward with God that is to be found by meeting him in secret at the center of our being.

CHAPTER XIII

THE INNER ROOM
AND THE LORD'S PRAYER

❦

Having discussed secret acts of charity and the centered place from which they spring, Jesus begins to discuss the second context in which perfection is to be expressed in the sixth chapter of Matthew, verses five and six. In these verses he says:

> And when you pray, you are not to be as the hypocrites; for they love to stand and pray in the synagogues and on the street corners, in order to be seen by men. Truly I say to you, they have their reward in full. But you, when you pray, go into your inner room, and when you have shut your door, pray to your Father who is in secret, and your Father who sees in secret will repay you (Mt 6.5,6).

The same hypocrites who gave gifts in the synagogues and distributed water in the streets to be noticed by men would also pray elaborate prayers in the synagogues and on the street corners in order to be noticed by others. However, having said that those men will have their appropriate reward, Jesus demands that his disciples pray in a different way, telling them to go into their inner rooms and to find God in the secret place where a divine reward will become accessible.

What is this inner room to which Jesus refers and the secret place to which he wishes to give us access? As a child, I found a room of this kind when I saw my father early one morning, kneeling in prayer at a window with a large downy blanket wrapped around him. I quite naturally identified the act with the room, for so early in the morning it was clearly intended to be a private, even secret, place. However, I soon began to sense that the secret place was not the room, but the center of the person in the room seeking communion with God.[1] It is a commonplace of psychological theory that a house is an image of the person who lives in it, and in many passages of Scripture the word "house" is used to call our attention to the person who is to be found there. Where then is the secret room within the house if it is not the centered place within the soul where one meets God face to face? As Kierkegaard saw so clearly, the centered self is defined in relation to an Other, and that Other is divine perfection that attempts to express itself through us.[2] Moreover, as Augustine suggests again and again, the problem of self-definition is not to be resolved by bringing God into relation with us, but by finding him present already at the center of our being. When we are far away from him, he is never far from us, and it is the inner room which Jesus mentions here that serves to give us access to him.[3]

In verses seven and eight of Chapter Six, Jesus elaborates his teaching about the inner room by contrasting his injunction to find it with a second kind of praying which he finds unacceptable:

> And when you are praying, do not use meaningless repetition, as the Gentiles do, for they suppose that they will be heard for their many words. Therefore do not be like them; for your Father knows what you need, before you ask Him (Mt 6.7,8).

Such prayers are composed largely of phrases strung together from the past, and it is phrases of this kind to which Jesus refers in the words "meaningless repetition." These meaningless repetitions are not unintelligible, but are meaningless simply because they combine words that were once alive into sentences that have lost their original power. Words of this kind are utterly ineffectual, and Jesus warns his followers never to use them. Jesus also warns us not to think that we will be heard because we use many words, for it is not the function of prayer to inform God of a situation about which he would otherwise be ignorant. God is closer to us than we are to ourselves, and Jesus emphasizes this fact by reminding his disciples that their Father already knows what they need before they ask him. God knows what we need before we ask because he already stands at the center of human existence, and it is this centered place that he asks us to enter in this passage. Whatever the words may be, the point of prayer is to make it possible for us to move to the place where God is. And when this occurs, the inner room becomes a secret, centered place where God is already waiting to respond.

When the inner room has been transformed into a secret place, and when the secret place has become the centered place, the question quite naturally rises: How do we pray? If prayer has this centering function, and if it need not involve many words that are intended to persuade God to come to us, how should we proceed? Though this question is not formulated in Matthew's version of the Sermon, it does occur in Luke, where having reached this decisive stage of the discussion the disciples say, "Lord, teach us to pray" (Lk 11.1). If we interpolate this request into Matthew's account, we find Jesus' response to it in verses nine through thirteen of Chapter Six:

> Pray, then, in this way:
>> "Our Father who art in heaven,
>> Hallowed be Thy name.
>> "Thy kingdom come.
>> Thy will be done,
>> On earth as it is in heaven.
>> "Give us this day our daily bread.
>> "And forgive us our debts,
>>   as we also have forgiven our debtors.
>> "And do not lead us into temptation,
>>   but deliver us from evil.
>>   [For Thine is the kingdom, and the power,
>>   and the glory, forever. Amen]" (Mt 6.9–13).

The first thing to notice about this prayer, which is usually called "The Lord's Prayer," is that it is not so much his prayer as ours. This is not primarily a prayer that Jesus prays, but rather, a prayer he teaches his followers to pray. Thus, "The Lord's Prayer" should be understood as the prayer Jesus has taught us to pray. Jesus himself has a prayer that is recorded in the seventeenth chapter of John and that occurs at the penultimate stage of his journey toward the cross (Jn 17.1–26). This prayer stretches across twenty-six verses, and it exhibits four characteristics. In the first place, it is a prayer of glorification, or more appropriately, a prayer that calls our attention to God's perfection and to the perfection Jesus shares with him. In the second place, it is a prayer of intercession in which Jesus asks his Father to unify his followers and to allow them to share his divine perfection. In the third place, it is a prayer of sanctification in which Jesus asks the Father to protect and separate his disciples from evil. And finally, it is a prayer that extends these requests to us, asking that all who believe in him be included within the kingdom he has come to make accessible.

There is, however, a second prayer—not his but ours—which is the prayer he has taught us to pray; and its purpose is to lead us into the perfection that God has already displayed as it is expressed in the seventeenth chapter of John. How then does Jesus begin in verse nine of the chapter before us? In this context he says, "Pray then in this way: 'Our Father who art in heaven, hallowed be Thy name.'" The first phrase, "pray, then," is in the imperative mood and thus constitutes a command to his followers; but the command also suggests that the prayer Jesus will teach his followers involves a pattern that he intends for prayer to follow. He not only says, "Pray," but also "Pray according to this pattern," and he begins to express the pattern he has in mind in the remainder of verse nine in the words, "Our Father who art in heaven, hallowed be Thy name."

The word "Father" is absolutely essential in the prayer Jesus teaches his followers, for the first thing he is trying to teach them is that prayer must always be directed to the Father. When we pray, we must pray according to a pattern, and that pattern begins by addressing God directly. It is quite true that prayer involves the Son and the Spirit as well, but the initial focus of prayer is the Father whose perfection Jesus has come to reflect. When we pray, we turn directly to God, and no human being or human institution is to serve as mediator. In another context Jesus tells us that when we turn directly to the Father, we go to him *through the Son,* for as he says in the

fourteenth chapter of John, we are to pray to the Father in his name
(Jn 14.13,14). Thus, our prayers begin with a reference to the Father
and end with the phrase, "In Jesus' name." But if prayers are directed
to the Father through the Son, Paul makes it clear in the book of
Ephesians that they are also uttered in the power of the Holy Spirit
(Eph 6.18). Thus, the goal and the initial direction of prayer is the
Father; the pathway of prayer is the Son; and the source of power
that allows us to make contact with God when we pray is the presence of the Holy Spirit.

It is important to notice that Jesus' use of the word "Father" in
this context involves a radical departure from the Old Testament
tradition. In fact, only rarely, if ever, does the Hebrew tradition refer
to God as "Father." The two most important words for "God" in
Hebrew are not even vaguely approximated by the English word
"Father." For example, the word "Elohim" involves such majestic
transcendence that the concept of "Father" as a translation of it
would be completely inappropriate (Gn 33.20). And the word "Yahweh," which was used when Moses encountered God at the burning
bush, invokes such mystery that the Jews have always refused even
to utter it (Ex 3.14).[4] Thus, when Jesus tells us to begin "The Lord's
Prayer" with the phrase, "Our Father," he is departing from what
the Hebrew tradition would have originally suggested. However, in
this departure from tradition, he is reflecting his own experience of
God as Father in what has often been called the "Abba! Father!"
experience of Jesus (Mk 14.36).[5] Thus, Jesus tells his followers that
he wants us to begin our prayers with the word that characterizes his
own relation to God.

A word like "Father" is richer in its connotations than we have
yet been able to suggest, and when it is used in its richest sense the
word reverberates with the powerful and awesome presence of God.
This dimension of the word is expressed on all those occasions where
Jesus says, "I have come into the world so that the perfection of the
Father can be revealed" (Jn 12.46). Jesus stands related to a Father
who displays awesome majesty and who reveals himself as the abysmal ground and the sustaining source of human existence. On the
other hand, the paradox of this relation is that the awesome mystery

and the tremendous power of the word before us also point to a place where the most intimate affection can be found, and it is into this place that Jesus is attempting to lead us when he says "When you pray, say, 'Our Father.'"

It is important to notice that at the beginning of the prayer we have not just one word, but two, and that Jesus not only says "Father" but rather "Our Father." His original utterance serves to bind us both to God and to one another, which is of course one explanation for the fact that we often pray "The Lord's Prayer" together. Yet we must not forget that we do not share this status as children of God simply because of creation, for as Paul says in the third chapter of Galatians: "You are all children of God through faith in Christ Jesus" (Gal 3.26). Thus, when we pray "The Lord's Prayer," we must not only be clear about the One to whom it is directed and about the community it invokes, but also about the fact that this community is constituted by an act of faith that allows us all to stand on common ground. There is no reason to confuse the two senses in which God is our Father, for though there is a sense in which he is our Father through creation, he is our Father more fundamentally through an act of redemption.

The first verse of "The Lord's Prayer" which begins with the words, "Our Father," ends with the phrase, "Who art in heaven, hallowed be Thy name." If the reference to the Father and to the "Abba! Father!" experience that Jesus wants to share with his followers brings closeness, reassurance, confidence, and community, it nevertheless remains true that God never loses his awesome majesty. The transition from "Our Father" to "in heaven" and "hallowed" interjects a sacred dimension into our response to him, and places our experience of God as Father back within its cosmic context. The source of confidence that binds us together is also an expression of the holiness of God, and as a result, the ground of comfort and reassurance is the divine perfection without which any attempt to address God as Father would degenerate into a mere triviality.

Having pointed to the heavens, Jesus quickly brings us back to the earth by also telling us to pray, "Thy kingdom come, Thy will be done, on earth as it is in heaven" (Mt 6.10). Having allowed us to reach what lies beyond, where the majesty of the one who can also be addressed as Father is to be encountered, Jesus returns us to the real order and asks us to pray for the day when the contrast between the heaven and the earth will finally be obliterated. It might appear that Jesus is asking his disciples to pray that what is true of heaven will be true of earth, and that it will be true here and now. However, most scholars agree that this admonition is intended to call our attention to an eschatological moment when the kingdom will come and when the new heaven and the new earth of John's apocalyptic vision will finally be revealed. Thus having focused our attention upon the Father in heaven, Jesus asks us to pray for the eschatological realization of divine perfection on the earth.[6]

At this point Jesus turns to the task of making provision for the here and now in which his followers are immersed and about which they are often far too preoccupied. Thus, in verse eleven he tells them to pray: "Give us this day our daily bread" (Mt 6.11). In the prayer Jesus teaches us to pray, he first speaks about what lies beyond, then speaks about the end, and finally, speaks about what is to be expected in between. It has often been pointed out that the translators of this passage have a difficult time rendering the phrase "daily bread," for this is the only occurrence of this expression to be found in the New Testament. Moreover, the term does not occur in any other literature of the period, allowing us to understand it by comparing it with its use in these other contexts. However, archaeologists were able to shed light upon the problem when they unearthed a tablet written in Aramaic that appeared to be a grocery list, and upon which this word occurred in a conspicuous place. In this case, the context suggested the translation "daily bread." But the really crucial problem of translating this expression has to do, not with the word "bread," but with the adjective that qualifies it. We might be inclined to believe that the entire sentence should be rendered, "give us *this* day's bread," or perhaps "give us *every* day's bread," but I find more striking the suggestion that the sentence should in fact be translated, "give us *tomorrow's* bread *today*." In what respect does this translation serve to advance our discussion, and how does it enable us to understand the structure of the here and now, standing in between the heavens with which we begin and the end toward which we look?

We might think that the "here and now" is constituted simply by "this day," without reference to a day beyond, in which case the sentence before us should be translated "give us *this* day's bread." Or we might attempt to protect our present situation against any possible encroachment, so that the relevant translation becomes, "Give us this day *every* day's bread." But could it perhaps be the case that Jesus is trying to place his followers in between this day and every day, asking us to live in between utter anxiety and satisfied self-sufficiency. When we pray, "Give us today *tomorrow's* bread," we do not ask for the absolute fulfillment that can be achieved only when the kingdom comes. On the other hand, we are not left isolated within a single day without some thrust toward the future into which Jesus wishes to lead us. We often move back and forth between absolute fragmentation and the wish for a guaranteed result, but the gospel invariably attempts to place us somewhere in between. Thus, the sentence before us becomes, "Give us this day tomorrow's bread," thereby enabling us to stand in between the anxiety we dread and the kingdom we will one day inherit.

Notice also verse twelve, where Jesus asks us to pray, "Forgive us our debts, as we also have forgiven our debtors" (Mt 6.12). The word translated "debt" in this context points in two directions: first to monetary debt, and then to moral debts that can be equated with our sins. In fact, the parallel passage in Luke uses the word "sins," making it explicit that we are asking for forgiveness for our separation from God (Lk 11.4). The word *"indebted"* in Matthew also implies that the debt is so serious that it can never be repaid by our own efforts and that we are asking to be forgiven for an utterly bankrupt condition. Yet this radical interpretation also has a positive role, for it will enable us to understand the second clause of verse twelve where Jesus says: "as we have forgiven our debtors." It is tempting to believe that Jesus is asking us first to forgive our debtors, and that having done that, God will then forgive us. However, the structure of the verse as a whole suggests that we are not being asked to forgive others as a *condition* for being forgiven, but that an analogy is to be found between divine forgiveness and those situations in which we have forgiven others. As a result, verse twelve becomes "Forgive us our bankrupt condition, as we, by analogy, have sometimes forgiven the debts of others."

Having spoken about forgiveness, Jesus brings the original version of "The Lord's Prayer" to a conclusion in verse thirteen with the words: "Do not lead us into temptation, but deliver us from evil" (Mt 6.13). There are two words in Greek that are sometimes translated "temptation," and in order to understand this passage, it is important to distinguish them. One of the words can be translated "temptation," but the other word which is to be found in this passage can be rendered more accurately as "testing." Therefore, the more accurate translation becomes "lead us not into testing, but deliver us from evil." In the first chapter of James, verses thirteen through fifteen, the writer says that God is not the source of temptation. If the Scriptures are consistent, Jesus cannot be telling his disciples to ask the Father not to lead them into temptation, and indeed, he does not do so, since the word translated "temptation" here differs from the word James uses in the first chapter of his book. As James himself says, the source of temptation is the evil one, and it is from this source that Jesus encourages his disciples to ask for deliverance. Therefore, verse thirteen can be paraphrased as follows: "Lead us not into testing, and also deliver us from the evil one who is the source of temptation."

Though God is not the source of temptation, he is the source of testing, and we have a classic illustration of this in the Old Testament tradition, where the Scripture says, "And Abraham was tested" (Gn 22.1). What, then, is Jesus' intention here with respect to his disciples? The key to the verse lies in the phrase "lead us not *into* testing," for the preposition in this sentence is very strong, expressing the fear that we might be led into a context where the pressure becomes so great that we will lose sight of our ultimate source of deliverance. The verse before us therefore calls our attention, not to temptation, but to the testing context in which a mature mode of existence can be established. And the request being made in this verse is that we not be led so deeply into the wilderness that we forget the salvation that will come when evil has finally been conquered.

At the end of verse thirteen, we find a clause that is not part of the original text, though I do not for a moment propose that in saying "The Lord's Prayer" these words be eliminated. That beautiful conclusion reads: "For thine is the kingdom, and the power, and the glory, forever. Amen." One of the purposes of Matthew's gospel was to provide material for worship in the early church, and from a rhetorical point of view, it is easy to understand why this concluding phrase was added in later manuscripts.[7] These words mediate the abruptness of the phrase "deliver us from evil," and they reflect the larger intentions of the Sermon on the Mount, even though they are not part of the original text. The kingdom referred to here is the kingdom that has been mentioned earlier in the prayer; the power in question is the power that grounds the earlier part of the message; and the glory mentioned at the end is the perfection to which the kingdom and the power that express it finally point. "The Lord's Prayer" begins with the Father and points beyond the human realm to the heavenly region he inhabits; it moves back to the earth and points to the end when it says, "Thy kingdom come, thy will be done, on earth as it is in heaven." It then places us in between absolute insecurity and complacent self-sufficiency by saying, "Give us today tomorrow's bread," and having asked for forgiveness, it asks that we not be led so deeply into testing that we lose sight of deliverance. Finally, having taken us back into eternity with the words, "For thine is the kingdom, and the power, and the glory, forever," it concludes with the word "Amen," which to a Hebrew audience simply means that we believe and are committed to the words that have just been uttered.

In bringing our discussion of "The Lord's Prayer" to a conclusion, we turn finally to verses fourteen and fifteen, which are not part of the prayer itself, but which serve to develop one of its crucial implications. In these verses Jesus says:

> For if you forgive men for their transgressions, your heavenly Father will also forgive you. But if you do not forgive men, then your Father will not forgive your transgressions (Mt 6.14,15).

It is with reference to this passage that our earlier discussion of the problem of debts and forgiveness becomes relevant, for the word which points to bankruptcy and is translated "debt" in verse twelve differs from the word rendered "transgressions" in the passage before us. The word "transgressions" refers to sins that are committed *after* our bankrupt condition has been forgiven, and with reference to sins of this kind Jesus suggests, "If you will forgive others their transgressions, I will forgive yours; but if you will not, I will not forgive yours because I cannot, since fellowship with me depends upon living within a community where transgressions are forgiven." What is under discussion here is not salvation, or the claim that our access to it depends upon our willingness to forgive. Rather, what is in question is the existence of a Christian community, the condition for which is a life of mutual forgiveness. What are we to do about the transgressions we commit after we have become citizens of God's kingdom and about the sins of others to be encountered in this same context? In these concluding verses Jesus tells us that we must forgive, for it is only if we do so that he will forgive us and make accessible what David described in the Psalms as "the joy of our salvation" (Ps 51.12).

CHAPTER XIV

FASTING AS A CENTERED ACT

❦

At the end of the fifth chapter of Matthew, Jesus calls his disciples to a life of perfection, and as we found in our earlier discussion, the perfection in question is to be understood in terms of the concept of maturity. Jesus did not expect his followers to transcend the pressures of ordinary human existence, but he also knew that if he was to build his kingdom, it was vitally important for them to reach the maturity into which they had been called. Thus, in the concluding verse of Chapter Five, Jesus says, "Therefore you are to be perfect, as your heavenly Father is perfect."

Having spoken about the need for Christian maturity in general terms, Jesus does not leave the matter there, but turns instead to six specific contexts in which perfection ought to be expressed. The first involves acts of charity and the second acts of prayer, but in both of these contexts, the structure of the discussion is identical. In each case, Jesus distinguishes between acts that are performed in order to be noticed by others and acts that emerge from the center of human existence. In the first case, the acts in question are degenerations of the kind of life Jesus asks his followers to embrace, while in the second they put us in touch with the secret place where the perfection of God is to be found. As Jesus formulates the point with respect to giving and praying: when these acts are performed in secret, our Father who sees in secret will meet us there and will reward us appropriately. Jesus confronts his followers with the contrast between human fragmentation and human wholeness, and he suggests that fragmentation can be transformed into unity only if we move beyond religious externality into the hidden place where God himself is to be found.[1]

Jesus turns to the third context in which he asks us to express divine perfection in verses sixteen through eighteen of the sixth chapter of Matthew. In these verses he focuses upon the Jewish concept of fasting, and with respect to it he says:

> And whenever you fast, do not put on a gloomy face as the hypocrites do, for they neglect their appearance in order to be seen fasting by men. Truly I say to you, they have their reward in full. But you, when you fast, anoint your head, and wash your face so that you may not be seen fasting by men, but by your Father who is in secret; and your Father who sees in secret will repay you (Mt 6.16–18).

In this passage, Jesus suggests that fasting resembles giving and praying, and that it can be done either to be noticed by others or as a centered act that expresses the core of human existence. Yet he also elaborates the content of this specific example by drawing us a verbal picture of how people appear when they fast from these distinguishable points of view. What can be said about those who fast in order to be noticed? They put on the gloomiest face imaginable, they make certain that their clothing is in radical disarray, and they disfigure their faces, either by permanent or impermanent marks that obscure their appearance. By contrast, Jesus tells his followers that when they fast, they should anoint their heads and wash their faces so that their secret acts will not be noticed, but will enable them to receive a divine reward.

It is tempting for the religious consciousness to believe that spiritual existence must be disfigured or distorted and that one of its fundamental purposes must be to attract the attention of others. By contrast, Jesus suggests that the life of the spirit is symbolized best by anointing our heads and washing our faces. Anointing the head with oil was the classical Hebrew symbol for the presence of God's spirit within, and washing was the symbol for the cleansed soul that was the precondition for a transformed life. In fact, in Chapter Thirty-six of his prophetic book, the prophet Ezekiel describes both dimensions of Jesus' instructions to his disciples in spiritual terms:

> Then I will sprinkle clean water on you, and you will be clean; I will cleanse you from all your filthiness and from all your idols. Moreover, I will give you a new heart and put a new spirit within you; and I will remove the heart of stone from your flesh and give you a heart of flesh. And I will put My Spirit within you and cause you to walk in My statutes, and you will be careful to observe My ordinances (Ez 36.25–27).

In our contemporary culture, fasting is not as familiar a part of customary religious activity as giving and praying, and as a result, it is important to emphasize the fact that fasting was a regular part of the religious activity of Jesus' own day. Jesus is addressing an audience to whom the act of fasting was familiar and who needed specific advice about how to proceed with respect to it. However, since fasting no longer stands at the center of the contemporary religious consciousness, several questions arise about it, the first of which pertains to how fasting itself can be characterized. The typical answer to this question is to say that fasting consists in giving up food or drink for a limited period of time and replacing it with activities that have an essentially spiritual significance. When fasting is defined in this way, and when one engages in it in these terms, there are a number of psychological consequences that result which are valuable in their own right and which serve to accomplish the larger spiritual purposes which the act of fasting is intended to achieve. Anyone who has fasted knows that first there is a moment of emptiness, then a moment of despair, and that only after one has moved beyond these stages does he achieve the spiritual transformation for which the act of fasting is intended. Moreover, it is only in this transformed state, and only having endured both emptiness and despair, that one begins to locate the center of the centered self.

However, there is a more profound dimension of the act of fasting than this, and if we fail to come to terms with it, we will have missed Jesus' point entirely. Originally, fasting was not engaged in deliberately, but as a response to an intense, personal, and even overwhelming experience of either joy or grief, the reaction to which led quite naturally to a refusal to eat or drink.[2] The further consequence of an experience of this kind, so moving and profound, was that in undergoing it, one quite naturally began to neglect his appearance. Jesus knew that fasting often occurred in this way, and for very profound reasons, but in this passage he merely calls our attention to this fact indirectly by rejecting the pharisaical degeneration of the phenomenon in question. Knowing that fasting originally involved a kind of behavior that stemmed from a powerful personal experience, the imitator, lacking an experience of this kind, deliberately put on a gloomy face and neglected his appearance in order to be noticed by men, imitating the joy or the anguish that can only emerge from the center of human existence. In recommending that his disciples anoint their heads and wash their faces before they fast, Jesus is asking them to distinguish themselves from the hypocrites who are engaged in merely imitative behavior. As a result, we are confronted once more with a picture of two distinguishable modes of existence: one on the rim, one at the core; one on the outside, one within; one on the circumference, and one at the center. It is this distinction that Jesus has been concerned to draw throughout this section of his teaching, and it is this contrast that he has in mind when he discusses the problem of fasting.

There is one further transition that needs to be made if we are to understand the richness of Jesus' intentions. Knowing that fasting originally expressed a centered act, Jesus takes that act to a still higher level of spiritual development by suggesting that it is possible to fast, not simply because our joy or grief forces us to do so, but also as a deliberate expression of the human desire to find God.[3] In his advice to his disciples, Jesus points to this higher level of development by asking his disciples to anoint their heads, to wash their faces, and to fast in order to embrace a positive encounter with God that subordinates everything else to itself. In this case, fasting is not to be undertaken as a psychological or spiritual experiment, endured as a natural consequence of an overwhelming personal experience, or flaunted as a way of imitating a centered act that is thrust upon us, but becomes instead a deliberate act in which we focus voluntarily upon the single overriding objective to commune with God, causing everything else to pale into insignificance in comparison with it. Jesus implies that it is only when fasting is done for this reason that it can display more than a merely episodic significance.

My great-grandmother, whom I never saw and never knew, was an invalid, but the most important fact about her life was that she fasted once a week. She studied the passage before us very carefully, and every Wednesday she anointed her head, washed her face, and fasted all day in her room. Though she would allow people to visit her and would willingly converse with them during the day, the point of her activity was not to be noticed, but to be absolutely committed to a single overriding spiritual objective. In her case that overriding objective was this: though she was unable to leave her room, and though in a certain sense she was imprisoned behind closed doors, she sought to reach the center of her being where God was to be found, and from there to reach out beyond herself to make living contact with the larger world. When as a little boy my father would visit her on Wednesdays, he became aware of her powerful presence and by being there was given access to the secret place where God himself reveals his richness. He says that one day in the midst of their conversation his grandmother said to him, "Son, there are more prayers stored up for you in heaven from this room than you will ever be able to use." Later on as a mature man he began to realize that for her, fasting was not an experiment, not a reaction to an overwhelming experience of joy or grief, not a merely external act that was performed in order to be noticed, but an attempt to embrace a single objective which was to find the center of human existence and to pray for both her grandson and for the larger world from that perspective. Because she did that, she was able to speak to a little boy who came to talk to her, and by implication, also spoke to me and to those who read these pages. Thus, Jesus tells us that in addition to giving and praying, there is a third context in which divine perfection can be expressed, and as my great grandmother discovered, it is within this context that both giving and praying can display one of their richest manifestations.

CHAPTER XV

TWO TREASURES, TWO WAYS OF SEEING, TWO MASTERS

❦

The fourth context in which Jesus asks his followers to express divine perfection exhibits three distinguishable dimensions, the first of which is expressed in verses nineteen through twenty-one of Chapter Six. In this passage, Jesus says:

> Do not lay up for yourselves treasures upon earth, where moth and rust destroy, and where thieves break in and steal. But lay up for yourselves treasures in heaven, where neither moth nor rust destroys, and where thieves do not break in or steal; for where your treasure is, there will your heart be also (Mt 6.19–21).

Most commentators suggest that the key to these verses is to be found in the phrase "lay up treasures *for yourselves*" and that the central claim being made here is not about treasures, but about the purpose for which they are intended. According to this interpretation, Jesus is warning his disciples against laying up treasures for themselves, where their own private satisfaction becomes the guiding principle of their existence.[1] However, a crucial distinction is also being drawn in these verses between two places where treasures can be located, one of which is upon the earth and the other of which is in heaven. In the first case, moths attack from the outside and the result is holes within; our

140

treasures left to themselves begin to rust and corrode; and when the moths and the rust have done their work, thieves break in and steal our possessions. Even if we were able to patch the holes and polish the rusted treasure, it would still be possible for a thief to steal it altogether, leaving us not simply with mended garments or with polished metal, but with absolutely nothing.[2] By contrast, Jesus refers in the second case to "treasures in heaven," where moth and rust do not corrupt and where thieves do not break in and steal. And he implies that treasures of this kind are to be located in a secret place where we meet God face to face.

The clearest indication that Jesus has the inner room of our earlier discussion in mind in this passage is to be found in verse twenty-one of Chapter Six where he says: "for where your treasure is, there will your heart be also." In the Bible a reference to the heart is a way of calling our attention to the center of human existence, and as a result, this verse suggests that we are confronted with a choice between two distinguishable orientations. If we choose to lay up treasures in heaven, we find the secret place where God appears, and the center of our own lives is brought into a direct correlation with the ground of life itself. But if we choose the earth instead, and if our existence finally comes to focus there, we discover that our lives are lived on the circumference, where corruption and emptiness are the ultimate result. According to this passage, the chief question to be considered is whether our hearts coincide with the divine perfection we are asked to embrace, or whether we will fall away from it, allowing the focus of our existence to be defined in merely peripheral terms. In speaking about laying up treasures on the earth, Jesus is implying that it is possible for human existence to degenerate, while in pointing to the possibility of laying up treasures in heaven, he suggests that the purpose of life can be found only by bringing our hearts into a positive relationship with God.

One of the classical expressions of the distinction between the two places where our treasure can be located is to be found in the story about the Fall of Lucifer. When Lucifer attempts to become divine, he storms the gates of heaven in order to place himself at the center of God's kingdom. When he does so, he is immediately cast back to the earth and is forced to live there, accumulating what earthly treasures he can as the temporary ruler of it. Both the temporary status and the degenerate character of the treasure Lucifer embraces are suggested by the Biblical prophecy that he will one day be placed in chains at the center of the earth he is attempting to master. In this case, being chained in an earthly abyss becomes an eschatological expression of radical degeneration, while access to the kingdom of heaven remains accessible only for those who bring their hearts into accord with God's divine perfection.

When I was a child, I knew a man and his wife who had no children, and when my parents would leave town for several days, I would sometimes stay with them. Despite the radical difference in our ages, we were very close, and it is this fact that gives this story its special poignancy. As the years went by, my friends became relatively wealthy, for the man had a good job, both he and his wife inherited a great deal of money, and they both made some very wise investments, one of which was in a business in the town where we lived. When I came home for a visit from graduate school one year, my father told me that one of the saddest things that had happened during the past year was that my friend's business had been robbed during the day while he was there, and that it had been a very traumatic experience for him, especially since he had now become an elderly man. I responded by going down to the business to visit, and went into my friend's office to speak to him. However, when I looked in on him, he was sitting behind his desk, counting the money that had been collected that day and poring over his account books as he mumbled to himself.

I tried to speak to him four times, but I never got his attention. He had been losing his hearing for a number of years, and perhaps I should have spoken a bit louder or walked over to put my hand on his shoulder. However, I left without making any contact with a friend I had known for many years. When I got back home, I told my parents about the episode, and they reminded me that he was still afraid because of the robbery and feared that something similar might happen again. However, the heartbreaking fact about what I had seen was that my friend's attention was so captivated by the treasure spread out before him that he was unable to respond to human contact. "Do not lay up for yourselves treasures upon earth," Jesus says, "where moths and rust destroy and where thieves break in and steal, but lay up for yourselves treasures in heaven. . . ." Of course, it is quite possible that we will sometimes possess some earthly treasures that are worth displaying from a human point of view. However, it is absolutely essential that these earthly treasures be a context where divine perfection can express itself rather than a finite resting place that is finally subject to corruption and emptiness.

At this point, let us turn to verses twenty-two and twenty-three, where we find a distinction between two kinds of vision corresponding to the original contrast between two kinds of treasure. In these verses Jesus says:

> The lamp of the body is the eye; if therefore your eye is clear, your whole body will be full of light. But if your eye is bad, your whole body will be full of darkness. If therefore the light that is in you is darkness, how great is the darkness! (Mt 6.22,23).

The distinction in verse twenty-two is between two ways of seeing, one clear and the other distorted. The word translated "bad" in this context is to be rendered literally "folded over." The image evoked is the contrast between an eye that is clear and unobstructed and one that is defective and has an eyelid folded over it for compensation. When a garment has a defect, we may attempt to mend it by folding a piece of good cloth over the flawed material. In a similar way, the contrast Jesus has in mind in this passage is the distinction between clarity of vision and an eye whose defect is so radical that we attempt to camouflage the fact by folding an eyelid over it. The contrast before us is not simply the distinction between clear and defective vision, but the much more radical distinction between eyes that are open and eyes that are covered over to hide the original defect. In this case, the defectiveness of the vision is compounded by a vain attempt to remedy the original problem so that the defect becomes doubly negative.

Within the context of the Sermon on the Mount, another alternative is always open to us. When our vision is clear, the light can shine in; and when our eyes are defective, it is possible for us to pray the prayer that God will always hear: "Lord, be merciful to me a sinner" (Lk 18.13). The tragedy of the case before us is that instead of praying that prayer, we get needle and thread to sew a good eyelid over a bad eye in order both to hide and remedy our defect, and in doing so, our defective eye is covered over so completely that no light can ever penetrate our darkness. And as Jesus himself suggests at the conclusion of verse twenty-three, "when darkness of this kind is present, how great is that darkness." The light that Jesus wants to bring to clear eyes is sometimes met by the defectiveness of our distorted condition, and it is dark when that is the case. But it is not as radically dark as things become when with mending tools in hand, we cover the defect over and no light is allowed to enter at all. Light can still penetrate an eye that is simply distorted, but covering over our defective vision with an eyelid through which we are unable to see separates us from the light altogether.

There is one further point that needs to be made in this connection, and this crucial point is that clarity of vision is part of the divine perfection into which Jesus is attempting to lead his followers. Spiritual existence should not be confused with emotional exuberance and is perfectly compatible with absolute clarity of vision about the most important questions. Of course, the vision in question is not the kind of perception that merely sorts and measures, but the kind that allows the light to become visible and that permits us to speak about it in the most coherent and persuasive terms possible. Jesus himself attempts to do this in his teaching, and it is the clarity of vision that he commends to his followers that allows teaching of this kind to occur.

Finally, in verse twenty-four of Chapter Six we reach the summarizing sentence in which Jesus brings this portion of the Sermon on the Mount to a conclusion. In this verse he says:

> No one can serve two masters; for either he will hate the one and love the other, or he will hold to one and despise the other. You cannot serve God and mammon (Mt 6.24).

We might be tempted to resolve the problem of the two ways we can seek perfection by merging them, refusing to acknowledge the incompatibility between heavenly and earthly treasures and between clear and obstructed vision. Jesus anticipates this attempted resolution, and in response to it, he tells us that we must choose between two radically distinct modes of existence. He does not simply say that we should not serve two masters, but says instead that we *cannot,* implying that doing so is a logical impossibility.[3] We attempt to lay up treasures in two directions; we attempt to embrace two ways of seeing; and in the process, we attempt to serve two masters. However, Jesus insists that a choice between these two ways of life is forced upon us and that it is ultimately impossible to deny the claim that we can only serve a single master.

In discussing this point in his book about the Sermon on the Mount, E. Stanley Jones says that this demand of Jesus is inescapable, whether we are rich or poor. Jones spent his life as a missionary in India, and he was absorbed by the problem of poverty he confronted there. Yet he tells a story about a woman caught on an island in a flood, dressed in rags and holding a sack of potatoes in her hands. The potatoes were not simply to be used as food, but were for purposes of barter as well so that the distressed woman was holding all the "money" she possessed in her hands. As the rescue boat approached, those in it reached over the side to help her in; but at the decisive moment, she drew back, clutching the sack of potatoes rather than the hand that could take her to safety. As the boat departed and as the waves rolled in, she finally discovered the awful truth in Jesus' words that we are unable to serve two masters.[4]

CHAPTER XVI

BEYOND ANXIETY

❦

In the first eighteen verses of the sixth chapter of Matthew, Jesus distinguishes between two kinds of giving, two kinds of praying, and two kinds of fasting; and in all three of these cases, he tells us that the fundamental contrast is the same. On the one hand, we can give or pray or fast in order to be noticed by others; while on the other, we can do these things in secret where God himself both sees and promises to reward us. Jesus poses a choice for his followers between two modes of existence and between two places where our action can originate: one on the surface and one at the center; one at the periphery and one in the middle; one in public view and the other in the private place where God himself is to be found. In each case the alternative he asks us to embrace is clear. Yet having distinguished between seen and being noticed, Jesus also draws a threefold distinction between two kinds of treasure, two kinds of vision, and two kinds of master, and in this case he suggests once more that the focus of our attention should be oriented toward the ground of human existence (Mt 6.19–24). If we take seriously his claim that it is impossible to serve two masters, the distinction before us is not simply a contrast between two possibilities, but becomes a distinction between two ways of living, one of which must be chosen in clear and radical opposition to the other.

Jesus presupposes that the disciples he is addressing have already chosen a master to follow, and he begins verse twenty-five with this assumption. In this verse he says:

146

For this reason I say to you, do not be anxious for your life, as to what you shall eat or what you shall drink; nor for your body, as to what you shall put on. Is not life more than food, and the body than clothing? (Mt 6.25).

The first phrase of this passage points to the presupposition that his disciples have made an initial commitment to him and are prepared to act on his claim that a choice must be made between two kinds of master. However, it is also appropriate that he address the problem of anxiety at this point, for it is at this place that even his closest followers must confront the most difficult questions of human existence. There are at least two reasons why anxiety is such a central problem, the first of which is a reflection of its radical indeterminacy. Anxiety sometimes becomes so penetrating because its vague and indeterminate character makes it difficult if not impossible to bring it to determinate focus. In this connection, a distinction is usually drawn between fear and anxiety, where fear has a definite object while the state of anxiety does not. In the first case, the remedy for our predicament is clear, at least in principle, while in the second it remains unclear, precisely because of the unfocused character of the problem. The second reason anxiety is such a difficult problem is connected with the first, for its indeterminate character allows it to become a pervasive dimension of the human soul. Anxiety threatens to invade the center of human existence, and as a result, it is important that the one who wants to meet us there should address this problem directly.

The pervasive and the indeterminate dimensions of anxiety that most of us experience sometimes spring from the divided consciousness that Jesus has been attempting to make whole. What makes us anxious? One of the things that does so is our tendency to embrace two incompatible ways of living which are expressed in two kinds of giving, two kinds of praying, two kinds of fasting, and which are also exemplified in two kinds of treasure, two ways of seeing, and two kinds of master. When we refuse to make a choice between these alternatives, anxiety begins to do its work, breaking apart the center of human existence into a cluster of fragments. Jesus confronts the problem of anxiety at this point, because it is the place where we find the fundamental antithesis to the unified and centered self. Jesus also has a task for his disciples to perform, but he knows that they will never succeed in performing it if anxiety distorts the wholeness to which he wishes to give them access. The fundamental problem of the human soul is the conflict of the soul with itself as it makes its choice between fragmentation and unity.[1] Thus Jesus asks his followers to make this choice decisively by demanding that they not be anxious for their lives, either with respect to what they eat, or drink, or with regard to the clothing they might wear in order to disguise their fragmented condition.

As we focus on verse twenty-five in more detail, it is important to notice that Jesus does not attempt to replace the anxiety we might experience about external things with a higher anxiety about the soul. Jesus never claims that the solution to the problem of the anxious soul is to turn away from anxiety about the bodily dimensions of existence so that we can express anxiety about more important matters.[2] In this respect, the crucial words in the text are body and soul, soma and psuche, and Jesus says that anxiety is utterly inappropriate in both cases. As he formulates the point more specifically, we should not be anxious about the body with respect to clothing, but should also not be anxious about the soul with respect to food and drink. The concept of the soul in the Greek text points to the animating principle in virtue of which the person is a living being, and Jesus warns his followers that anxiety even within this "spiritual" context ought to be avoided. Thus he concludes verse twenty-five with the rhetorical question, "Is not the soul more than food, and the body than clothing?"

But what is the additional dimension to which Jesus points when he asks his followers about this something more? As the passage before us will make clear, Jesus wants them to focus their attention upon God's kingdom which transcends both the external and internal dimensions of human existence. If we are to find God at the center of life, we will not do so by succumbing to anxieties that affect either the body or the soul, but only by being oriented toward the kingdom of God and toward the divine righteousness he makes accessible. In fact, Jesus suggests how this orientation can be established by asking a further series of questions, each of which comes to focus on a concrete example of the grace of God. In verses twenty-six through thirty he says:

Look at the birds of the air, that they do not sow, neither do they reap, nor gather into barns, and yet your heavenly Father feeds them. Are you not worth much more than they? And which of you by being anxious can add a single cubit to his life's span? And why are you anxious about clothing? Observe how the lilies of the field grow; they do not toil nor do they spin, yet I say to you that even Solomon in all his glory did not clothe himself like one of these. But if God so arrays the grass of the field, which is alive today and tomorrow is thrown into the furnace, will He not much more do so for you, O men of little faith? (Mt 6.26–30).

The first example Jesus chooses calls our attention to the birds of the air, the most important fact about which is that they fly in and through the medium God meant them to occupy. They are not dislocated in the order of things; they remain within the medium in which they were designed to move; and as long as this is so, Jesus tells us that God will care for them.[3] Unfortunately, the example would not have been necessary unless our own situation had been so different. There is indeed a place where God meant for us to be, and this place is to be found when we respond to God's grace. However, in sowing, reaping, and harvesting, we sometimes move from the center to the surface of life, displaying the anxiety that often accompanies a dislocation of this kind. The distinction between the anxious soul and the centered soul becomes, by analogy, the distinction between a bird occupying the place it was meant to inhabit and a bird dislocated. In our own case, this dislocation takes the form of moving from the center to the circumference of existence, where this transition expresses itself in the anxiety of the fragmented soul. In comparing our anxious situation with the relative security of a bird, Jesus is also careful to say that *we are worth more than they*. He not only refuses to transmute external anxiety into anxiety about the soul as an animating principle, but also insists upon referring to the order of nature as an appropriately hierarchical arrangement.

The point of Jesus' example about the birds of the air is not to express a romantic conception of nature, but to point to the ground of existence that sustains the natural order. In claiming that we are worth more than animals, he is suggesting that we can be even more intimately related to God than creatures that are lower in the order of nature. However, the tragic fact is that unlike the birds, we sometimes fall away from God so that our self-conscious participation in the ground of existence is displaced by an indeterminate and pervasive anxiety. In fact, one of the explanations for our capacity to turn away from the center of our existence is the dimension of self-consciousness that makes us superior to the animals. We are worth more than the birds because of our capacity to say yes or no with respect to the fundamental issues of life. Our greater worth is therefore related to our volitional capacity to respond to God, which in turn forces us to confront the problem of anxiety as a human possibility. The world Jesus describes is not a seamless fabric, and one indication of this fact is his willingness to ascribe greater worth to human beings than he does to animals. The paradox of Jesus' words is that the world is also divided at a higher level by our capacity to turn away from God and to be overtaken by anxiety that can fragment the human soul. It is this kind of anxiety from which Jesus asks his followers to turn away, suggesting that if God feeds the birds of the air, he is also prepared to take care of his children.

Notice how Jesus continues to address the problem of anxiety in the rhetorical question of verse twenty-seven: "Which of you by being anxious can add a single cubit to his height?" Or in another possible translation of the same passage, "Which of you can add a single cubit to his life's span?" Let us consider both translations as legitimate ways of expressing Jesus' intentions. The common thread in both cases is our incapacity to transcend our natural limitations, but when both translations are considered our attention is also directed to the two regions where we live and about which our anxiety is most frequently expressed. Jesus' question at this juncture implicates both space and time, and when both translations are brought together, he says by implication: "Do not be anxious, for anxiety will not add a single cubit to your height, nor will it add anything to the temporal spread of your existence." The two ways in which we exist—both spatially and temporally—cannot be augmented by the anxiety under discussion. The anxious soul often attempts to do this by transcending the finitude of its natural situation. Anxiety about our stature and anxiety about the future can be understood as expressions of our wish for absolute security and of our reluctance to live within our natural limitations as they are grounded in the grace of God. In this passage, Jesus reminds us of our finitude, and suggests that anxiety is never an adequate way of responding to it.

In the first three chapters of Genesis, the story of the Fall is an account of the refusal of the human being to acknowledge and accept his limitations. Satan had already attempted to storm the gates of heaven and to become God, and when he failed, he came to the garden of Paradise to tempt the woman to imitate his failure. And what does he choose to whisper in her ear? "I was not content with my limitations, and look how beautiful I have become by attempting to transcend them. Why don't you do the same, so that you also can become like God?" But what was the natural consequence of the woman's act? Adam and Eve ate the forbidden fruit and fell away from the center of human existence, condemned from that moment to earn their bread by "the sweat of their brows." As the story of Genesis also suggests, the anxiety of the trembling heart was the natural result, for expulsion from the garden placed the man and the woman at a great distance from the original harmony they had been created to express. By contrast, Jesus tells his followers that even though they are finite, God will care for them, and that by implication, the anxiety of the Fall should be replaced by faith in him. Jesus wants his followers to find a unified existence in the midst of finitude, and instead of being anxious about our spatial and temporal limitations, he wants us to discover what the Apostle Paul described as God's strength undergirding our weakness (2 Cor 12.9,10).

Jesus continues to make this point in verses twenty-eight through thirty in terms of another example. The same themes that are present in the earlier discussion are also to be found here. In this passage Jesus suggests that his followers should not be anxious about their clothing, and he implies that God is prepared to care for them in an even richer way than he does for the lilies of the field. In turning his attention from food to clothing, he turns back from the soul to the body, suggesting that having promised to feed the soul, he will also care for the external dimensions of existence. Yet at a deeper level, the example of the lilies serves to bring both the internal and external dimensions of human life

together. The lily grows from the inside, and its external beauty is
simply a manifestation of its intrinsic nature.[4] Jesus tells his disciples
that they need not be anxious about the external dimension of existence, for as in the case of the lilies, the center of their existence can
flower forth into a rich external manifestation. The crucial task once
more is to find God at the core of our existence and to overcome
anxiety about the body and the soul in terms of the power to be found
there, and the crucial word that gives us access to power of this kind is
to be found at the end of verse thirty where Jesus says, "O men of little
faith." Faith stands in direct correlation with the grace of God, and
both internal and external growth are a direct reflection of its strength.
In fact, the metaphors that are used in the Scriptures to express the
concept of faith often invoke the contrast between an open and a
closed heart. Thus, it is not surprising that the conquest of the anxiety
that often engulfs and encloses us is expressed in this passage in terms
of the concept of faith.

The focus of the faith to which Jesus refers at the end of verse
thirty becomes clear in verses thirty-one through thirty-four:

> Do not be anxious then, saying "What shall we eat?" or "What shall
> we drink" or "With what shall we clothe ourselves?" For all these
> things the Gentiles eagerly seek; for your heavenly Father knows
> that you need all these things. But seek first His kingdom and His
> righteousness; and all these things shall be added to you. Therefore
> do not be anxious for tomorrow; for tomorrow will care for itself.
> Each day has enough trouble of its own (Mt 6.31–34).

Notice first that the things about which he asks us not to be anxious
pertain once more to the soul and the body—what we eat, what we
drink, and what we wear. Jesus says that anxieties of this kind should
be avoided because the Gentiles seek such things eagerly, thereby
placing a concern with them at the foundation of human existence.
The Gentiles to whom Jesus refers in this passage know nothing about
the grace of God, and they have therefore never made the transition
from an infinite but futile quest for satisfaction to faith in God. In
asking his disciples to embrace a life of faith, Jesus reminds them that
their "heavenly Father" already knows their basic needs and that it is

absolutely unnecessary to allow anxiety about them to define the character of their quest for fulfillment.

Jesus quickly elaborates a positive alternative to this degenerate mode of existence when he says to his disciples: "Seek first His kingdom and His righteousness, and all these things shall be added to you." The command to seek God's kingdom first gives it priority with respect to both time and value, and it turns our attention away from peripheral considerations to the center of life where God himself is to be found. Jesus also suggests that when we find the kingdom of heaven, the righteousness of God becomes accessible, and our natural quest for a satisfaction of our own will be replaced by a different kind of journey that will satisfy our basic needs. The paradox of this passage is to be found in the fact that though both kinds of journey begin with a quest for satisfaction, the first fails and the second succeeds because of the different kinds of power displayed by their objects. Food, drink, and clothing can only satisfy our natural desires through consumption, while a quest for God brings satisfaction by making it possible for us to receive a divine gift. The quest for wholeness that is oriented toward God inverts the natural consciousness, and it puts us in touch with a source of power that will both transcend and satisfy natural desire.[5]

The possibility of natural satisfaction is expressed at the conclusion of verse thirty-three, where Jesus promises that if his followers will seek God's kingdom and his righteousness first, "all these [other] things will be added to you." The things about which we were anxious at the beginning will be added at the end, and this is so because they will be the natural result of our having finally located a divine kingdom. This does not mean that we will be utterly free of discord and that difficulties about the ordinary dimensions of existence will never need to be confronted. However, it does mean that if we seek God first, the other things about which we might be anxious will ultimately be made accessible. Unfortunately, it is also true that if we seek those other things with all our hearts, the center of life will never be found; for to seek satisfaction on the periphery of human existence will ultimately explode the centered self. Jesus asks his followers to choose between two ways of life, one of which unifies the spirit and

also allows our natural desires to be satisfied, while the other fragments the soul and enmeshes us in a cluster of anxieties that can never
be assuaged.

Jesus brings his discussion of anxiety to a conclusion in verse
thirty-four where he says: "Therefore do not be anxious for tomorrow; for tomorrow will care for itself. Each day has enough trouble of
its own." Anxiety often expresses itself in temporal terms, and concern about what we will eat or drink and about what we will wear are
frequently expressions of our anxiety about what might happen tomorrow. We want to guarantee the future, and anxiety reveals its
essential nature in our desperate attempts to do so. However, Jesus
reminds us that every day has troubles of its own and that those should
be dealt with independently of our anxious projections about problems that might arise tomorrow. When we deal with problems today
in their appropriately bounded and finite context, and when we do so
in the light of our prayer that God will give us tomorrow's bread
today, we will find the center of life where God speaks. The question
Jesus poses for his followers is a question about two ways of life, one
of which is overwhelmed by anxiety and the other of which is sustained by his infinite power. And it is finally in terms of this trans-
forming power that he intends to lead us beyond anxiety.

CHAPTER XVII

JUDGMENT AND CONDEMNATION

❦

In this chapter we turn to verses one through six of the seventh chapter of Matthew, where Jesus brings his discussion of the six regions where divine perfection can be expressed to a conclusion. Having claimed in Chapter Five that his disciples should be perfect as their Father in heaven is perfect, he illustrates the point with respect to giving, praying, and fasting; elaborates it further with respect to two kinds of treasure, two ways of seeing, and two kinds of master; and then focuses our attention upon the pervasive problem of anxiety, suggesting that perfection can be achieved only by embracing a divine kingdom where God himself is to be found. Jesus summarizes this crucial point by telling his followers to seek God's kingdom and his righteousness first, and he says that if they do so, all their practical concerns will also be dealt with appropriately. However, there is one final context where perfection is demanded, but where those who have experienced it and wish to express it are especially vulnerable. This dimension of the discussion pertains to the problem of judgment and condemnation, and a warning about it is formulated in verses one and two of Chapter Seven:

> Do not judge lest you be judged. For in the way you judge, you will be judged; and by your standard of measure, it will be measured to you (Mt 7.1,2).

The first thing to notice about this warning is that the crucial verb upon which it depends is in the present tense, the active voice, and the imperative mood. As we have discovered already, the present tense in the Greek text implies duration or continuous action *over an indefinite period of time*. Unlike the present tense in English, which often calls our attention to a specific moment, the Greek present points to a series of moments that can stretch out over a lifetime. Thus, when Jesus says, "Judge not . . . ," the claim being made is that we are to refrain from judgment, not only now, but also tomorrow, and into the indefinite future within which the pattern of a new way of life is to be expressed. The active voice suggests that this pattern is to be established by us, and that the one to whom the original injunction is addressed must decide whether he will act on the command that Jesus has expressed. However, the most important fact about the verb in question is not its tense nor its voice, but the fact that it is spoken in the imperative mood. The form of the verb makes it clear that the followers of Jesus are not being given an option, but a command, and this command is expressed as a prohibition against judgment.

If the sentence, "Do not judge lest you be judged yourselves" is expressed in the form of a command that suggests that the entire pattern of human existence is at stake, the word in question has several uses that must be distinguished clearly. In the first place, a judgment can be a simple assertion of the sort, "I judge that the chair is to the left of the table." In this case, a judgment is expressed simply by uttering a declarative sentence. In the second place, a judgment can express an act of appraisal in which one claims that something is valuable or that one thing is worth more than another. Judgments of this kind are an inescapable aspect of human existence, and they reflect the need to make evaluations before appropriate courses of action can be undertaken. In fact, even assertive judgments display an evaluative dimension, at least in the sense that an assertion implies that what has been asserted is true. Truth is one of the things we value, and it is this fact that allows an assertion to be evaluated with respect to its truth or falsity. There is also a third place where the concept of judgment plays a crucial role, and it is this third context that Jesus has in mind most clearly in this passage. Sometimes a judgment involves a self-righteous criticism of others designed to express condemnation, which implies that the one who makes the judgment is vastly superior to the person he condemns, and it is a judgment of this kind that Jesus condemns in this passage. Though Jesus allows his followers to make assertions and appraisals, he demands that they turn away from self-righteous criticism and condemnation.

Why does Jesus focus his attention upon judgment at this point, and why does he wish to warn his followers to turn away from it? What is wrong with judgment understood as condemnation, and why will it undermine the kingdom Jesus is attempting to develop more quickly than almost any other kind of behavior? The answer to the first question is that judgment of this kind is a typical expression of the self-righteous satisfaction that can result from a direct encounter with God, and the answer to the second is that the ecstasy and liberation of such an experience can easily generate a feeling of superiority that will ultimately fragment the Christian community. It is a great paradox that self-righteousness should sometimes be the consequence of gaining entrance into God's kingdom, and it is a paradox equally surprising that the church where redemption should be at the center so often becomes a place where condemnation is the definitive condition. Jesus knows that his followers will be inclined to transmute divine perfection into self-righteous superiority, and as a result, he chooses to focus on the problem of condemnation at this point.

One of the principle characteristics of self-righteous condemnation is that it often says more about the one who makes the criticism than it does about its target. The Apostle Paul knew this very clearly, for as a brilliant product of a proud tradition, he grappled very seriously with the problem of self-righteousness. In the midst of lengthy accounts of his sufferings for the cause of Christ, he would often remember his illustrious heritage, and it was no doubt difficult for this "Hebrew of the Hebrews" to accept the discord and the persecution with which he was sometimes confronted (Phil 3.5). However, in the second chapter of the Book of Romans he echoes the warning of Jesus when he says:

> Therefore you are without excuse, every man of you who passes judgment, for in that you judge another, you condemn yourself; for you who judge practice the same things (Rom 2.1).

What are the characteristics of others that we are most inclined to criticize and condemn? As Paul suggests, it is surely those things that we also find within our own souls. Jesus warns his followers that if they are to express divine perfection, they must turn away from self-righteous criticism of others and come to grips with their own souls.

Jesus gives this warning to his followers because he knows that the criticism of others often occurs in inverse proportion to one's own spiritual condition. At the end of the day, when my own critical thoughts about my colleagues sometimes begin to dominate my thinking, and when I am most preoccupied with all the difficulties they have caused that seem to warrant condemnation, I almost inevitably find that my own spiritual condition has degenerated in the process. In fact, there is a familiar episode in Scripture that reflects a similar predicament and that can serve as the prototype of our own problems in this connection. John the Baptist, who had baptized Jesus and who had pointed forward so persistently to his coming, was thrown into prison toward the end of his life by Herod, the tetrarch of Galilee (Mt 4.12). Suffering there in despair and in the face of impending death, he sent a message to Jesus saying, "Are you the Coming One, or shall we look for another?" (Mt 11.1–3). Of course, there is an implicit criticism hidden there, but the criticism reflects more about the temporary condition of John than it does about the one toward whom it is directed. Thus, Jesus warns his followers that divine perfection can be expressed only if we turn away from condemnation.

In verse two of Chapter Seven, Jesus also tells us that when we judge another in order to condemn, the same kind of judgment will be directed toward us, and according to the same standards we have already employed. A farmer was once standing beside the road when two travelers passed by. The first traveler was trying to decide whether he should settle down in the town up the road. The farmer very wisely said to him, "What kind of people were in the town where you lived before?" "Oh," the traveler said, "it was the worst town imaginable; there was bitterness, adultery, gossiping, discord, and worst of all, insincerity among the so-called religious people living there." The farmer replied, "All things considered, I think it would be best if you not stop in this town because it is the same kind of place." However, when the second traveler asked the same question, and when the farmer asked him about his past, the traveler replied, "The people where I lived before had their faults as most of us do, but they were sometimes kind and sympathetic, and from time to time love could be found there. In fact, all things considered, I would say that it was a grand place to live." This time the farmer said, "I believe you will be happy here, for that is exactly the sort of town we have here."[1] Thus Jesus says, "Judge not . . . , for in the way you judge you will be judged, and by your standard of measure it shall be measured to you."

There is another important point to be considered about the problem of judgment which might easily be overlooked. Before we judge in order to condemn, we should at least consider the possibility that no one but God can know enough about the concrete situation of another to pass a judgment of this kind. It is easy to assume that we know all there is to know about someone else's situation and that because of this fact, we are uniquely situated to pass judgment upon it. However, the circumstances of others are often so different than we imagine and sometimes so complicated that our external perspective can never do justice to it. In such circumstances, it is far more appropriate to inquire about the source of another person's problem than to pass critical judgment upon him, finally choosing to leave the task of judgment in this sense to God. But what is the standard that God uses when he passes judgments of his own? This is the question that Paul, haunted by the overpowering force of the law and burdened by the guilt of his sin, often put to himself. In Chapter Seven of the Book of Romans, Paul describes the internal oppositions and the discordant elements of the human soul; and he cries out from the depth of his being:

> For the good that I wish, I do not do; but I practice the very evil that I do not wish. But if I am doing the very thing I do not wish, I am no longer the one doing it, but sin which dwells in me (Rom 7.19,20).

> Wretched man that I am! Who will set me free from the body of this death? (Rom 7.24).

But finally, having expressed his inner turmoil and having focused on the dimension of his soul that deserved condemnation, he finds wholeness in Christ and concludes in verse one of Chapter Eight: "There is therefore now no condemnation for those who are in Christ Jesus." If it is the case that condemnation is to be repudiated, and if in the final analysis judgment of this kind ought to be left to God, the last word of the gospel to a suffering world that is caught in the conflict of criticism and mutual condemnation is the word that comes to us from an Apostle who had understood his master. With respect to the problem of judgment, the Apostle says that there is no condemnation for those who have chosen to respond to the message of Jesus.

In verses three through five of Chapter Seven, Jesus begins to elaborate his original warning about judgment in the following way:

> And why do you look at the speck that is in your brother's eye, but do not notice the log that is in your own eye? Or how can you say to your brother, "Let me take the speck out of your eye," and behold, the log is in your own eye? You hypocrite, first take the log out of your own eye, and then you will see clearly to take the speck out of your brother's eye (Mt 7.3–5).

The first thing to notice about this passage is the tendency it identifies to judge in two directions or in accord with two relatively distinguishable standards. We judge ourselves by one standard, and others by a standard that is very different.[2] We have already suggested that condemnation of another can be a reflection of one's own self-condemnation, but when self-condemnation occurs, it is often unconscious and is therefore prone to focus its attention upon another. In fact, the more I condemn myself unconsciously, the more severe my criticism of others, and the more I criticize another, the more often a disparity exists between the explicit standard I apply to myself and the standard I employ in judging others. Judgment of another is often the externalization of an inner cauldron, and it is this predicament that Jesus addresses when he demands that we remove the beam from our own eye before we provide a remedy for the speck in the eye of another.

In verse three, the word translated "*look* at the speck in your brother's eye" is "*blepo*" and is rendered more adequately, "glance superficially out of the corner of your eye." Though we are prepared to deal with the defects of others in accord with the most rigorous standards, we often do so after only a superficial glance and in utter disregard of the massive defect in ourselves from which the drive toward condemnation often springs. Jesus is attempting to remind his followers that taking specks out of other people's eyes is a delicate operation and that it is not to be performed with a sledgehammer! He suggests that it can be performed properly only when one has raised a prior question about one's own condition and has dealt with it appropriately. It is sometimes necessary to remove the speck in the eye of another, and Jesus never suggests that operations of this kind are not sometimes appropriate. However, he does insist that critical self-appraisal is a necessary condition for operations of this kind to be successful. Unless we can see our own predicament clearly, we will never be able to see beyond it to the larger community we are asked to serve.

Jesus makes this point even more emphatically in verse five when he says, "You hypocrite, first take the log out of your own eye, and then you will see clearly to take the speck out of your brother's eye." Jesus tells us bluntly that we must first remove the log in our own eye if we are to see clearly in helping another person by removing the speck in his eye. It is interesting to notice that this passage suggests both the necessity and the possibility for a subtle shift in our attitude toward others. What began as self-righteous condemnation becomes a constructive operation if we have first come to terms with the fragmentation of our own souls. The removal of specks is part of the task to which Jesus has called his followers, and it is one of the ways in which he expects us to express divine perfection. But if this task is to be performed, self-condemnation and inner turmoil must first be overcome so that we can become appropriate vehicles for the constructive task of transformation.

We can summarize the teaching of verses one through five in this fashion: it is perfectly reasonable to make judgments, not only as assertions, but also as expressions of evaluation. But there is another kind of judgment which involves criticism and condemnation and from which Jesus asks his followers to turn away, for he knows that we will never be mature, or be what we were meant to become, until we come to terms with the fragmentation from which condemnation springs. He asks us to remove the log that is in our own eye, to recognize that we have been freed from condemnation, and to refrain from inflicting condemnation upon others. If God has removed condemnation with respect to the ultimate issues of life, we have no right to reinflict it upon others, but are asked instead to express constructive intentions when we remove specks from the eyes of others.

At the conclusion of this chapter, let me turn to verse six where we find a postscript that serves to bracket the previous discussion and to formulate a condition that must be met if divine perfection and Christian maturity are to be expressed appropriately. In this verse Jesus says:

> Do not give what is holy to dogs, and do not throw your pearls before swine, lest they trample them under their feet, and turn and tear you to pieces (Mt 7.6).

A number of suggestions have been made about how this passage should be interpreted, one of which is especially appealing to the symbolic consciousness of a contemporary audience. According to this alternative, Jesus is saying, "Do not give what is holy to the dogs of your desires, and do not throw your pearls before the swine of your appetites, lest those sides of yourself trample them under their feet and turn and tear you to pieces."[3] Despite the psychological insight that a reading of this kind displays, we should remember that in the New Testament, the word "dog" is almost always used to refer to Gentile unbelievers, the word "swine" refers to Jewish unbelievers, the word "holy" is used to set the life of the Christian apart from the world, and the word "pearl" is used to point to the possession of knowledge. If one will trace the relevant verses in which these words recur, "dog" means "Gentile," "swine" means "Hebrew," "holy" means "what is separated," and "pearls" means "the knowledge we have in our possession as a result of understanding the gospel." If we pursue this kind of interpretation, verse six says, "Do not give what is separated about the Christian community to the dogs, or the kind of knowledge required for maturity to the unbelieving world, whether Gentile or Hebrew: for if you begin in this way, you will invariably find that you will be trampled under the feet of those to whom you turn with this kind of teaching."

Where does Jesus want his disciples to begin in expressing divine perfection to an unbelieving world? With the Sermon on the Mount? With the claim that Jesus was one of the greatest teachers that the world has ever known? With the assertion that the ethical code he formulated is worthy of our obedience? Or with the claim that life will be enriched if we attempt to conform to the spirit of his teaching? Quite to the contrary, Jesus suggests that if we begin in this way, we will be trampled. In such a case, the Sermon on the Mount will become a set of ethical dicta within five minutes; the paradoxes will become unintelligible within ten; the life to which it leads, and the divine perfection it asks us to express will seem to be just the reverse; and the wisdom he wants us to embrace will appear to be utterly foolish. What then does Jesus expect us to say to lay the foundation for entrance into his kingdom? He expects us to claim that the only relevant condition for understanding his teaching is the self-conscious admission of one's own spiritual poverty which can be overcome only by God's grace. The Sermon on the Mount begins there, and until an audience is brought face to face with this fact, it is useless to proceed any further. When this initial point has been understood, the audience can then begin to develop toward perfection, and the "pearls of wisdom" to be found in the Sermon on the Mount can be understood and put into practice within the context of daily experience.

PART IV

FINAL CONSIDERATIONS ABOUT GOD'S KINGDOM

❧

CHAPTER XVIII

ACCESS TO DIVINE POWER

❦

The central theme of the Sermon on the Mount is to be found at the conclusion of the fifth chapter of Matthew, where Jesus tells his followers that he intends for them to become perfect just as their Father in heaven is perfect. As we have discovered in the course of our earlier discussion, the word translated "perfection" points to our need to develop toward Christian maturity. To be perfect is to be what we were meant to become; to be perfect is to be mature; to be perfect is to reach the stage of mature self-development that moves beyond the initial moment of Christian commitment into the fullness of life to which Christ is calling his followers. Having concluded Chapter Five with a command to embrace divine perfection, Jesus does not leave the matter there, but turns to six specific regions in which perfection or maturity can be expressed. He tells his followers that maturity is required within the context of giving; he says that it must also be embodied within the context of praying; and he claims that fasting is a further region in which God can be encountered and in which perfection can be expressed from the center of our being. Then Jesus speaks about two kinds of treasure, two ways of seeing, and two kinds of master, only one of which can be affirmed if mature self-development is to be achieved. Finally, Jesus tells us that maturity of this kind can express itself in two additional ways, which serve to bring the inner and the outer dimensions of human existence into a harmonious relationship. On the one hand he points to the possibility of a life that

transcends anxiety, and on the other hand, to a life that is not preoccupied with judging others because it has already experienced freedom
from condemnation in its own case. In all of these ways, he calls his
disciples to a life of divine perfection, where mature self-development
is to be forged within the concrete context of human existence.

After Jesus has pointed to the places where divine perfection is to
be reflected, a question quite naturally arises about how the source of
power is to be found that will enable us to express the perfection he has
asked us to embrace. As if he had anticipated an inevitable question,
Jesus begins to answer it in these words:

> Ask, and it shall be given to you; seek, and you shall find; knock,
> and it shall be opened to you. For everyone who asks receives, and
> he who seeks finds, and to him who knocks it shall be opened (Mt
> 7.7,8).

Jesus knows that his followers will confront concrete problems about
giving, praying, and fasting and that they will face inevitable choices
between two kinds of treasure, two ways of seeing, and two kinds of
master. He also knows that they will confront the problem of anxiety
and the problem of judging others, and that the more the level of
anxiety rises within, the more judgmental they are likely to become.
The question inevitably arises about where the source of power can be
found that will bring us back to the center of human existence from
which divine perfection can be expressed; and in verses seven and
eight, Jesus answers this question by saying that if we ask, seek, and
knock, the power we need will become available.

The tenses of the verbs in these two verses are of crucial significance, for as in so many cases, the Greek present of ask, seek, and
knock suggests continuous action stretched out over an extended
period of time. The verses in question tell us not simply to ask, but to
keep on asking; not simply to seek, but to keep on seeking; and when
we have finally reached the door, not simply to knock, but to keep on
knocking. The sustaining source of power that Jesus makes available is
not simply to be found in a momentary occurrence, but is given
instead to the follower for whom asking, seeking, and knocking have
become a part of the fabric of existence.

We must also notice that the continuous action expressed by this series of verbs is counterbalanced by the future tense conclusion of the clause in which they are embedded. As I have emphasized before, the future tense in Greek does not point so much to a future time, but to the absolute certainty of a logical consequence. Jesus not only says keep on asking, but also that the power we seek will be given; he not only says keep on seeking, but also that we will find what we seek; and finally, he not only tells us to keep on knocking, but also that the door before which we stand will be opened as a natural consequence. These verses suggest that the pattern of life being expressed here displays an increasing level of intensity and that the power we seek will be found only if this proves to be the case.[1] Divine power becomes accessible, not simply because asking, seeking, and knocking are stretched out over time, and not only because a divine gift, a divine discovery, and a divine self-disclosure are their natural and logical consequence, but also because the intensity of the power we need can be reflected in the intensity of the quest to find it. When the poverty-stricken spirit accepts God's divine gift, a process of self-development begins which can be satisfied only to the extent of the intensity of the human journey that seeks to embrace divine perfection.

In response to the claim that divine power is to be found in asking, seeking, and knocking, the question quite naturally arises: "What more specifically does God give us when asking, seeking, and knocking define the pattern of human existence?" On some occasions, we will be given what we ask, we will find what we seek, and we will receive what we knock for; but on other occasions, we will find—instead of what we ask—*what we most fundamentally need*.[2] If finding a source of divine power is required for achieving Christian maturity, we will not always find it by simply seeking what we want or even what we think we need. It is true that Jesus tells his followers in another context to come boldly before the throne of grace in time of need. Yet it remains the case that the boldness and the intensity of the human journey must be counterbalanced by the recognition that divine perfection is a gift and is not simply our natural possession. Thus, when we ask, seek, and knock, we should expect the answers we receive to be an expression of God's power and to be instances of

Jesus' earlier claim that the Father knows what we need before we ask. What God proposes to give us is his sustaining power, and this sometimes means that our specific requests must be transformed from what we want to what we need.

It is nevertheless true that these requests cannot remain vague and indeterminate, but must be made specific if mature self-development is to be achieved in concrete terms. Perfection is not an abstraction, and the sustaining power that makes it accessible must therefore express itself concretely in specific regions of human experience. Jesus has already pointed to those concrete places in his earlier discussion, and he has thereby given his followers guidance in their asking, their seeking, and their knocking. Jesus has discussed the question of maturity with reference to the question of giving, and therefore, it becomes appropriate for us to ask him, "Teach us how to give." He has also discussed the expression of divine perfection with respect to prayer, and therefore it becomes appropriate to ask, as his disciples did, "Lord, teach us to pray." Maturity can also express itself in the act of fasting, and thus we can ask, "How can I fast in such a way that my soul is centered and my mind is seeking God with such single-minded intensity that the rest of the world falls away?"

We have found that Jesus also distinguishes between two kinds of treasure, two ways of seeing, and two kinds of master, and he thus invites us to ask for treasures in heaven, for clarity of vision, and for a life of obedience to God, who is the only master worth serving. But finally he invites us to knock on the door of perfection and power so persistently that the anxiety which fragments the soul can be transcended and the judgmental tendencies we are so inclined to indulge can be outflanked. In giving us what we need instead of what we want, Jesus also leads us to the place where we can know what to ask, and where what we seek and find can be the expression of divine perfection in the world through us.

The specific contexts to which Jesus points in teaching his disciples what to ask can be embraced in one of two ways. As our earlier discussion suggests, there are two ways to give, two ways to pray, two ways to fast, two kinds of treasure, two ways of seeing, two kinds of master, and so on. If we are to ask, seek, and knock for divine power and perfection, only one of these ways can be embraced in each case, and that path leads us to the secret place where God himself is to be found. As a result, God not only wishes to give us what we need, but most fundamentally, he wants to give us himself. Keep on asking, keep on seeking, keep on knocking, Jesus says, and if we do so in accord with his instructions, we will find divine perfection as the focus of an otherwise fragmented life. From the moment in which we acknowledge our fragmented condition and enter God's kingdom, human wholeness becomes accessible to us. Yet there are a thousand fragments that still need to be gathered together if human life is to reach the perfection and the maturity for which it was intended. It is this maturity for which Jesus tells his followers to ask, seek, and knock, and he assures them that when they do so persistently, they will find satisfaction for their deepest cravings.

There is one final fact about the verbs of verses seven and eight that it is important to remember. If these verbs point from the side of the human realm toward continuous action, and if they point from the side of God toward absolute assurance, we must also notice that the verbs themselves are expressed in the passive voice. Ask and *it shall be given unto you*; seek and you shall find; knock and *it shall be opened unto you*. The implication is that the gift will be given and the door will be opened by a power that outstrips whatever power you or I can bring to bear upon our own fragmented condition. I cannot reach the center of my being by myself, and as a result, what is under discussion here is not simply a psychological act that seeks the pristine place where the winds that buffet us are to be transcended. Quite to the contrary, when we keep on asking, keep on seeking, and keep on knocking, we are seeking the perfection of God, and perfection of this kind can be found only when he opens the door.

In the Sermon on the Mount, the self is defined in direct correlation with God. Yet the quest for him will never reach its culmination apart from a final act of divine self-disclosure. It is a commonplace of philosophical psychology that the self is defined with reference to another. In fact, I can only say "I" when I can pronounce somebody else's name, and I can discover myself only through the mediation of another. But what is that Other to whom Jesus is calling our attention in this passage? He is the One who promises both to meet us at the center of our existence *and to define the center where we stand*. When we ask, when we seek, and when we knock, what we finally seek is God himself. Asking, seeking, and knocking is a process that requires the doorway to be opened by another. Thus Jesus says, "Ask and it shall be given to you; seek and you will find; knock and it shall be opened to you." When that door swings open because of God's power, we will be able to define ourselves for the first time, for the self will have been brought into a living relation with the sustaining ground of life itself.

It cannot be denied that asking, seeking, and knocking often display a great deal of psychological intensity and that this fact tempts us to storm the gates of heaven instead of allowing God to open them. In this case, God is not lost but simply displaced by our own infinite demands to achieve divine perfection for ourselves. The *only* self-defining being is a divine being, and this fact becomes a human problem because we are not only finite, but as made in God's image, infinite as well. We are both finite and infinite at once, and indeed, the passionate intensity with which we sometimes seek and knock is an expression of infinity. If we were only finite, we would not walk, or talk, or think, but would remain like the earthworm in an underground place where there is enough moisture. Because we are not simply finite but infinite as well, the natural consciousness attempts to explode beyond its finite limits, displacing our finitude with an infinite power of its own. The message of Jesus is that the infinite intensity of the quest for power and perfection can only be satisfied when it encounters the perfection and the power of God, and in the passage before us, that decisive moment occurs *when God himself opens the door*.

The power and the intensity of the act of asking for perfection must not be denigrated, and the erotic dimension of the human psyche which is manifested in our quest for perfection must never be canceled. However, Jesus himself has already said, "Seek first God's kingdom and his righteousness and all these *other* things will be added unto you." Only under the power of this guiding thread will all the fragments of a fragmented life be woven together, and this thread can be found only when God himself makes it accessible. We also find, paradoxically, that when the door swings open our infinity is affirmed and that anything is possible for those who have found God at the center of their existence. Find the center, and out of the power of that center *anything* is possible. In that moment, the infinite list of demands I make upon others and upon myself which can become so mesmerizing drops away, and my own infinite longings are transformed into an expression of divine power which God himself bestows as a gift.

In verses nine through eleven, Jesus brings the divine and human realms together and reasserts the primacy of God in terms of an analogy. In these verses he says:

> Or what man is there among you, when his son shall ask him for a loaf, will give him a stone? Or if he shall ask for a fish, he will not give him a snake, will he? If you then, being evil, know how to give good gifts to your children, how much more shall your Father who is in heaven give what is good to those who ask Him? (Mt 7.9–11).

The word "man" at the beginning of verse nine is "*anthropos*" and it means, of course, a man or a woman. There are two words in Greek that can be translated "man": one is *anthropos* and the other is *aner*. In this case we have "*anthropos*," which can be translated more neutrally as "human being." Thus Jesus says, "What human being among you, when he is asked for something by his children, gives a stone instead of bread?" Even in the natural consciousness—a picture of which we sketched out earlier—we find the tendency to give what is good to those who depend most directly upon us. For example, in the parent-child relationship, and in spite of our infinite quest for satisfaction, we want what is best for those who are dependent. Yet if this reversal of our natural desires is possible in the human realm, Jesus asks "how much more will our Father give good gifts to those who ask him." Asking, seeking, and knocking are not simply acts of our own, but acts through which we sometimes try to satisfy another, and Jesus assures us that God himself is even more prepared than we to satisfy the deepest longings of our souls. God wants us to live at the center of human existence, and when he opens the door, he bestows the gifts of his grace upon those who ask, seek, and knock.

In the version of the Sermon on the Mount to be found in the eleventh chapter of Luke, greater clarity is achieved about the content of God's gift than is apparent in the version before us. Matthew says simply, "How much more shall your Father who is in heaven give what is good to those who ask Him!" However, Luke renders the same thought in this slightly different form: "How much more shall your Father give the Holy Spirit to those who ask Him?" (Lk 11.13). At this point, we finally reach a richer identification of the source of power that sustains the followers of Jesus and makes Christian maturity possible, for Luke tells us that this source of power is to be found in God's life-giving Spirit.[3] The role of the spirit in human consciousness is to bring unity to an otherwise fragmented existence. The spiritual consciousness that has perfection as its goal is brought to greater unity by a power that works within; but Jesus tells us that in the final analysis, this state can be achieved only when the door opens, and when God gives us himself in the form of his Spirit.

CHAPTER XIX

THE GOLDEN RULE
AND THE NARROW GATE

❧

In the previous chapter we focused on the source of power that enables the disciples to embrace divine perfection, and we found that perfection of this kind becomes fully accessible only if we ask, if we seek, and if we knock for it. We also found that though we sometimes receive what we ask for, even when this proves not to be the case, we are always given what we need. Jesus has already suggested how some of our needs can be met by claiming that divine perfection expresses itself within the human realm, and that it can do so in the contexts of giving, praying, and fasting; in our choices between two kinds of treasure, two ways of seeing, and two kinds of master; and in the power to conquer anxiety and to transcend the judgmental tendencies that the fragmented soul often exhibits. If we are to ask for what we need, we must therefore ask for the power to act appropriately within all the regions of human experience where divine perfection can be expressed. In giving us what we need, and in giving us guidance about what we ask, God also gives us himself, and the Divine Spirit is the principle in terms of which the fragments of a fragmented life can be brought to unity. Jesus emphasizes the fact that we will be able to embody divine perfection only if we keep on asking, keep on seeking, and keep on knocking for it, and this goal will become visible only when the Spirit brings it to bear upon the concrete circumstances of human existence.

Having spoken about the gifts that God gives to those who ask him, Jesus turns in verse twelve to what appears to be a different theme. In this verse he formulates the Golden rule, and he does so in the following way: "Therefore whatever you want others to do for you, do so for them, for this is the Law and the Prophets" (Mt 7.12). However disconnected this formulation may seem to be from what has gone before, the word "therefore" suggests an intimate connection. In fact, the Golden Rule follows directly from Jesus' claim that God will give his followers the power to embrace the perfection they seek. The Golden Rule is not merely an ethical prescription, but is an expression of the power that brings unity to the soul, and it is finally in terms of this prior unity that we are able to do unto others what we would have them do unto us.

Though the Golden rule is connected with our earlier reference to the power of God's Spirit, it is also a way of bringing the discussion back into relation with the real order. Throughout the Sermon, Jesus moves back and forth between the centered place where divine perfection becomes accessible and the larger world to which it ought to be related. Thus, it is appropriate that having given us himself, he calls our attention to the human realm in which this gift can be expressed concretely. The principle before us is not simply an isolated ethical command, but is the guiding thread of the kind of life into which Jesus wishes to lead his followers. This life is an expression of the unity of the Divine Spirit, and it seeks unity for others just as it seeks it for itself. Jesus also tells us that this principle of unity is not new and that it simply summarizes the teaching of the Law and the Prophets. On other occasions, Jesus speaks about two great commandments, one of which refers to God and the other of which calls our attention to our neighbors (Mt 22.36–40). Here, he focuses only upon the second, but he does so by connecting it with the first by a "therefore." The power that brings unity and makes it possible to love God is now to be brought to bear upon the human situation, and it is unity of this kind which the Law, the Prophets, and the Golden Rule seek to establish in our relation with others.

There are two formulations of the Golden Rule to be found in the ancient world, one of which is embedded in an Eastern philosophical framework, and the other of which appears here as the distillation of the Hebrew tradition. The Eastern formulation is expressed in negative terms and asserts "Do not do unto others what you would not have them do unto you," while the formulation of Jesus is positive and declares "Do unto others what you would have them do unto you." The striking difference between the two formulations does not require detailed comment. The intention of the first is to bring order to human existence by restraining us from doing to others what we do not wish to have done to ourselves, while the intention of the second is to allow divine perfection to overflow into the world, doing unto others what we wish they would do for us. Indeed, the two formulations are not even logically equivalent at the descriptive level, much less as expressions of divine imperatives. The crucial point to notice once again is that the imperative of Jesus is formulated against the background of a prior unity and that it is intended to bring this unity to bear upon the larger world.

The positive formulation of the Golden Rule summarizes the teaching of the Law and the Prophets, but the principle itself is given new life by the content to be found in the Sermon on the Mount.[1] In describing the kind of life in which divine happiness is to be found, Jesus has already said that it is present in both the gentle and the merciful soul, and it is from gentleness and mercy of this kind that action for the benefit of others finally springs. If we are to find divine happiness, we will not do so within the strictures of the Law, but in the power of the Divine Spirit that brings unity to the soul and that allows this unity to be expressed to others. In the final analysis the Golden Rule is an expression of the grace of God. It is formulated on the basis of a divine gift; it presupposes the unity of the soul which the Divine Spirit makes accessible; and it acts to bring grace to others just as we want them to bring grace to us. The deepest longing of the human soul is to be dealt with in the light of the grace of God. Thus, Jesus suggests that having been given a divine gift, we should act gratuitously toward others, just as we wish their acts toward us would express the grace that God himself has already given. It cannot be denied that the human soul longs for order and that this quest for an orderly existence is expressed in the negative formulation of the principle before us. If we restrain ourselves from acting inappropriately, it might be the case that others will be willing to display a corresponding restraint. However, the deeper impulse of the soul is a positive reflection of God's own gratuitous acts, and it is a series of acts of this kind that Jesus asks us to display when he formulates the Golden Rule in positive terms.

In verses thirteen and fourteen of Chapter Seven, Jesus begins to summarize the way of life into which the Golden Rule, and indeed, the entire Sermon on the Mount are intended to lead us. In these verses he says:

> Enter by the narrow gate; for the gate is wide, and the way is broad that leads to destruction, and many are those who enter by it. For the gate is small, and the way is narrow that leads to life, and few are those who find it (Mt 7.13,14).

This brief passage takes us back to the beginning of the Sermon and reminds us of the condition that must be satisfied if we are to enter God's kingdom and if we are to move along the pathway that will finally lead us to divine perfection. At the beginning of his Sermon, Jesus said: "Blessed are the poor in spirit, for theirs is the kingdom of heaven." The implication of this claim is that when we approach the gate, our fullness must contract into emptiness if God is to give us access to divine happiness. In this context, Jesus formulates the same thought when he suggests that we can enter God's kingdom and live according to the grace reflected in the Golden Rule only if we enter by a narrow gate.

The verb with which verse thirteen begins is a divine imperative and is in the aorist tense, pointing to the fact that decisive action is demanded and that it must occur at a specific moment in time. Unlike the stretched out action required when we keep on asking, keep on seeking, and keep on knocking, entrance into the way of life that makes such persistence possible is momentary and must occur once for all. Divine happiness, and the grace of God that makes it possible, can become accessible in an instant, and the way of life to which they lead can then be developed over time as we persistently attempt to embody and reflect the perfection we have already encountered. We ask, seek, and knock for the complete actualization of the power we encounter when we enter the narrow gate, and as this power is expressed in the course of daily existence, we can begin to live according to the Golden Rule, the power of which is finally grounded in the grace of God. Thus Jesus reminds us of our need to re-embrace our spiritual bankruptcy, and having contracted to a point, to enter his kingdom at a specific moment and to enter through a narrow gate.

In verse fourteen, Jesus tells us that the gate we must enter is not only narrow, but is also small, and when these two facts are taken together, they suggest two things about those who wish to enter it. In the first place, every person who enters *must do so alone,* for the gate is wide enough for only one person at a time. We must respond to the command of Jesus for ourselves, and it is impossible for us to enter his kingdom as a part of a larger community defined in merely human terms. The moment of entrance into God's family is an individuating moment, and the larger community that will eventually develop is a function of the fact that each of its members has first stood alone. There is indeed a grand and glorious community waiting on the other side, and the richness of friendship it makes accessible transcends any other kind of relationship, genetic or otherwise. The entrance gate is not a gate through which the collective consciousness can pass, but requires a moment of radical individuation that each of us must be willing to embrace.

We must notice in the second place that we not only enter the narrow gate alone, but that its size demands that we bend over if we are to cross the threshold into a new way of life. However erect we may stand within the context of our ordinary situation, poverty of spirit is required before we can receive divine happiness and before we can stand erect within a divine realm. This poverty of spirit is expressed when we bend our natural consciousness to the demands Jesus makes in order that divine perfection can be bestowed upon us. The first summary statement of Jesus' teaching reminds us of the initial and decisive moment when we find a new way of life, and it does so by pointing to a gate that we must enter alone and to a posture that we must assume if our natural consciousness is to be inverted.

The gate Jesus asks his followers to enter opens out into a pathway, and it is this pathway that Jesus has been describing in the

Sermon on the Mount. His reference to a narrow gate not only returns us to the beginning of his message, but also reminds us of the journey we have to take and of the stages that the quest for Christian maturity must always display. As the Gospel of John would later formulate the point so forcefully, Christ himself is the gate and a response to his message of grace is a necessary condition for entrance into God's kingdom (Jn 10.7, 10.9). As Jesus himself emphasizes, the pathway into which he leads us is a narrow one, and discipline is required if we are to move from stage to stage along the way. The fact that the pathway is narrow does not mean that it is more difficult than other paths, but simply that it is not as wide as other ways of life that might be chosen.[2] In fact, Jesus himself refers to a wide gate and to a broad pathway that have difficulties of their own and that will finally lead us to destruction. By contrast, the pathway he asks us to follow leads us to the freedom of a disciplined life, and it is a life of this kind that will finally allow us to express divine perfection. Freedom is not to be identified with the apparent spontaneity and with the sheer diversity of a broad pathway, but with the focused and the orderly existence of the narrow way. The "method" of the Christian life, or as the term could be expressed more literally, the Christian "way of life," leads along a pathway that transcends the chaos of the broader way, and the disciplined freedom it requires gives us access to a source of life that sustains human existence.

In telling us that the narrow pathway of the Sermon on the Mount leads to life, Jesus does not intend to point simply to life as a biological phenomenon, but to life as the sustaining source of power that makes it possible for us to live. In this way, he calls our attention once more to divine perfection that seeks to express itself within the human realm and which will be able to do so if we walk along the path to which the Sermon on the Mount calls our attention. The source of life to which he refers in this passage is the same kind of life which he made accessible to the woman at the well in the Gospel of John and which he said would be a well of water springing up within the soul that followed him (Jn 4.5–26). The narrow way that Jesus asks his followers to enter not only brings life at the end, but also gives us access to life as living water, and it is this kind of life that sustains every step we take along the way. As Jesus formulated the point once more in the fourth gospel, "I am the way, the truth, and the source of life. No man comes to the Father but by me" (Jn 14.6). In this context, these words become, "My words in the Sermon on the Mount are the pathway; they give access to the truth that only a narrow way can make accessible; and when you enter the gate where I stand, you will find a sustaining source of life that will undergird the human journey."

There will always remain another possibility for human life, and Jesus reminds us of its existence by pointing to a wider gate and to a broader path, and by saying explicitly that only a few will find the narrow way. As Aristotle suggested, truth is one, error is many, and as a result, we should not be surprised that truth is often so difficult to find.[3] In the Sermon on the Mount, this difficulty is compounded by the fact that truth and life are made accessible as a gift, and by the further fact that receptivity to grace is a necessary condition for receiving them. The narrow gate and the narrow way are difficult to find because they require the inversion of the natural consciousness and receptivity to a source of life that wishes to express itself through us. The alternative to such a life, where the erotic consciousness seeks to express itself freely along a broad path, will never lead to the fulness it seeks. Jesus tells us that the wide gate and the broad pathway lead to destruction and that they do so as a natural result of the human quest for perfection. If we miss the narrow gate and the narrow path, we will miss the sustaining source of life, and if we choose the wide gate and the broad path, we will be destroyed, not by divine vengence, but by our insistence upon following a pathway of our own.

CHAPTER XX

WOLVES IN SHEEP'S CLOTHING

❧

Jesus tells his followers that having entered the narrow gate and having begun to move along a narrow pathway, they will find a source of life that will sustain every stage of the journey he has asked them to undertake. By contrast, he also calls our attention to a wider gate and to a broader path that many of those he encounters will find more attractive, and he warns us that this broader path will ultimately lead to destruction. Jesus also warns his disciples that discord will be encountered even along the narrow pathway, and he formulates this warning in verse fifteen of Chapter Seven in a reference to false prophets. In this passage Jesus says, "Beware of the false prophets, who come to you in sheep's clothing, but inwardly are ravenous wolves" (Mt 7.15). The tense of the verb Jesus chooses in this formulation does not point simply to a specific moment, but to a stretched out sequence of moments where vigilence is required. As we walk along the narrow path, he says that *we must constantly beware of false prophets,* or as he formulates the point in metaphorical terms, we must beware of "disguised wolves" that constitute a permanent threat.

The intention of the disguised wolf is to devour us, and a reference to wolves before an audience where some shepherds were no doubt present was in itself sufficient to mobilize a fear with which they were already familiar. However, the more serious threat to which Jesus refers in this passage arises from the disguise that the wolves to which he refers assume. When a wolf is encountered in his natural habitat, he often does not pose a threat at all, and even when he does, it is a straightforward expression of his nature that can be dealt with clearly and decisively. On the other hand, when a wolf puts on sheep's clothing, and when he disguises his intentions with an innocent countenance, the threat he poses is far more serious and insidious. As we move along the narrow path, the most serious problem to be confronted is not an encounter with evil that reveals itself as such, but the constant threat that malicious and destructive intentions will be hidden and that what might appear to be another sheep will be evil in disguise. Thus Jesus warns his followers about the threat of false prophets, who might appear to be pointing to a sustaining source of life, but who in fact want to divert us toward the broad pathway that leads to destruction.

Disguised wolves appear to walk along the same path which Jesus asks his followers to enter through a narrow gate. However, they appear along that path only to express hidden intentions and as a reflection of the fact that every genuine expression of divine perfection is always counterbalanced by a counterfeit coin. For example, in the eleventh chapter of II Corinthians, Paul refers to counterfeit apostles who are attempting to undermine his work and who are simply imitating his constructive intentions. In this passage, Paul says:

> But what I am doing, I will continue to do, that I may cut off opportunity from those who desire an opportunity to be regarded just as we are in the matter about which they are boasting. For such men are false apostles, deceitful workers, disguising themselves as apostles of Christ. And no wonder, for even Satan disguises himself as an angel of light. Therefore it is not surprising if his servents also disguise themselves as servants of righteousness; whose end shall be according to their deeds (2 Cor 11.12–15).

In verses three and four of this same chapter, Paul also refers to a counterfeit gospel which the false prophet will proclaim, and he does so once more by reminding us of the hidden satanic intention that such a gospel reflects:

> But I am afraid, lest as the serpent deceived Eve by his craftiness, your minds should be led astray from the simplicity and purity of

devotion to Christ. For if one comes and preaches another Jesus whom we have not preached, or you receive a different spirit which you have not received, or a different gospel which you have not accepted, you bear this beautifully (2 Cor 11.3,4).

And indeed, Jesus himself attacks the disguises of the Pharisees who masquerade as spiritual giants, but who mislead the sheep that he has come to shepherd. Thus Jesus says in the twenty-third chapter of Matthew:

The scribes and the Pharisees have seated themselves in the chair of Moses; therefore all that they tell you, do and observe, but do not do according to their deeds; for they say things, and do not do them. And they tie up heavy loads, and lay them on men's shoulders; but they themselves are unwilling to move them with so much as a finger. But they do all their deeds to be noticed by men; for they broaden their phylacteries, and lengthen the tassels of their garments. And they love the place of honor at banquets, and the chief seats in the synagogues, and respectful greetings in the market places, and being called by men, Rabbi. But do not be called Rabbi; for One is your Teacher, and you are all brothers (Mt 23.2–8).

But woe to you, scribes and Pharisees, hypocrites, because you shut off the kingdom of heaven from men; for you do not enter in yourselves, nor do you allow those who are entering to go in. . . . Woe to you, scribes and Pharisees, hypocrites, because you travel about on sea and land to make one proselyte; and when he becomes one, you make him twice as much a son of hell as yourselves (Mt 23.13, 15).

Woe to you, scribes and Pharisees, hypocrites! For you clean the outside of the cup and of the dish, but inside they are full of robbery and self-indulgence. You blind Pharisee, first clean the inside of the cup and of the dish, so that the outside of it may become clean also. Woe to you, scribes and Pharisees, hypocrites! For you are like whitewashed tombs which on the outside appear beautiful, but inside they are full of dead men's bones and all uncleanness. Even so you too outwardly appear righteous to men, but inwardly you are full of hypocrisy and lawlessness. Woe to you, scribes and Pharisees, hypocrites! For you build the tombs of the prophets and adorn the monuments of the righteous, and say, "If we had been living in the days of our fathers, we would not have been partners with them in shedding the blood of the prophets." Consequently you bear witness against yourselves, that you are sons of those who murdered the prophets. Fill up then the measure of the guilt of your fathers. You serpents, you brood of vipers, how shall you escape the sentence of hell? (Mt 23.25–33).

The smiling countenance of the disguised wolf, and the spiritual facade of the bankrupt life are the most serious threats that the follower of Jesus must confront as he moves along the narrow path. This is so, not simply because we might be misled by the disguise and follow a prophet who is not a sheep at all, but because the disguise masks a satanic intention. It is not by accident that Paul compares the disguise of the false apostle with the disguise of Satan as a messenger of light and with the satanic deception of Eve in the Garden, or that Jesus compares the deceptive Pharisees with vipers whose ultimate intention is to lead us to destruction. The false prophet, and false spirituality that disguises destructive intentions, are expressions of a primordial threat that those who walk along the narrow pathway must confront. Satan seeks to devour those who seek divine perfection because he wishes to glorify himself and to become divine as an expression of his own erotic power. He does not appear straightforwardly as a ravenous wolf that seeks to consume whatever blocks his quest for fulfillment, but rather disguises himself as an innocent sheep who must be led along the way by a shepherd who has already made the journey. If we are not constantly aware of the possibility of such a disguise, and if we follow the path along which these disguised intentions lead, we will be consumed by the same fire that will ultimately destroy the soul that attempts to achieve divine perfection by its own acts.

The story of the Garden of Eden to which Paul refers is the classic example of the primordial possibility of following the false prophet. Satan appears disguised as a beautiful creature, and his temptation consists in pointing to the possibility of a divinity that can result from a decisive human act. When this self-transcending act occurs, Adam and Eve recognize their own nakedness, and they attempt to camouflage their condition by sewing fig leaves together to cover their emptiness. When God comes walking in the Garden, and when they finally encounter him again, he takes the fig leaves from them and replaces them with a new garment of skin. This new garment that comes as a gift is the only satisfactory resolution for the human predicament, and it is finally this divine covering that enables them to walk along the narrow path. This makes any attempt to wear sheep's clothing as a disguise all the more dangerous and reprehensible, for it not only masks the satanic quest for divinity, but also imitates the gift that God alone can give.

When we approach the gate in our poverty-stricken condition, attempting to camouflage it with fig leaves, God gives us sheep's clothing. Yet he very wisely warns us to beware of wolves masquerading as sheep in order to recapitulate the satanic deception that led to our original predicament. If there is anything more vicious than the original satanic deception that provokes our natural quest for perfection, it is the subsequent deception that merely imitates the divine solution for our deepest problem, stitching a sheep's clothing over a ravenous and destructive intention. It is only when God provides the covering that a wolf can cease to be a sheep in disguise and can become a sheep indeed, and it is only then that the ravenous appetite can become the vehicle for divine power and can finally cease to be counterfeit coin.

What further guidance does Jesus give his followers about disguised wolves, and what does he suggest about how to recognize them and about their ultimate fate? In verses sixteen through twenty of Chapter Seven, Jesus answers these questions in the following way:

> You will know them by their fruits. Grapes are not gathered from thorn bushes, nor figs from thistles, are they? Even so, every good tree bears good fruit; but the bad tree bears bad fruit. A good tree cannot produce bad fruit, nor can a bad tree produce good fruit. Every tree that does not bear good fruit is cut down and thrown into the fire. So then, you will know them by their fruits (Mt 7.16–20).

In this passage, Jesus proposes a pragmatic test for unmasking hidden intentions, suggesting that the nature of a person's power and orientation is to be measured by its effects. Good fruit always comes from good trees and bad from bad, and it is ultimately this fact that will enable us to recognize the disguised wolf. This does not mean that the tree and the fruit it produces are identical, or that the goodness of the tree is simply to be equated with the goodness of its fruit. However, Jesus insists that we are able to understand the nature of a tree or a life, whose goodness or badness has already been established by its relationship with God, by observing the kind of fruit that tree or life produces. Finally, when a tree is destroyed, or when a disguised wolf is unmasked, this does not occur because the tree and the wolf do not bear good fruit, but because they are rotten and ravenous within. The destruction to which the broad pathway leads is not finally a function of what we do, but of who we are, and the fruits in each case are simply an external reflection of an internal condition. It is this internal condition that God wishes to transform, but if destruction finally comes, it will do so because the twistedness within which attempts to disguise its true nature will be identified as evil through the fruits it produces.

Perhaps an even stronger way to make this point is to suggest that a tree will be destroyed, not because it does not bear fruit, but because it is a rotten tree that is simply unable to be productive. Fruit flows from the center of a tree that is sustained by life-giving power, and the fruit from a life that travels along the narrow pathway is simply an expression of a divine source of power and perfection that springs up from within. When we meet the disguised wolf along the way, we can unmask its internal bankruptcy by observing the negative fruit it produces. Jesus also suggests that the real problem is not the masquerade, but the failure of the one who wears the mask to allow his life to be transformed by a divine gift. We are indeed to beware of false prophets and to unmask their disguises in terms of the kind of fruit they produce. However, the disguised wolf and the evil tree will be judged, not because of their disguises or their fruit, but because of the rottenness within that will always lead to destruction. The pragmatic maxim, "You shall know them by their fruits,"[1] is simply an external reflection of a more fundamental existential situation, and it is the situation that God himself will finally reward either in terms of life or in terms of destruction.

The final passage where Jesus discusses the possibility of divine rejection and the fate of the false prophets is to be found in Chapter Seven, verses twenty-one through twenty-three. In these verses he says:

> Not everyone who says to Me, "Lord, Lord," will enter the kingdom of heaven; but he who does the will of My Father who is in heaven. Many will say to Me on that day, "Lord, Lord, did we not prophesy in Your name, and in Your name cast our demons, and in Your name perform many miracles?" And then I will declare to them, "I never knew you; depart from me, you who practice lawlessness" (Mt 7.21–23).

What could possibly be lawless about prophecy in the name of Jesus, and what could be lawless about casting out demons and about performing miracles in his name? The only possible answer is that lawlessness of this kind results when one attempts to do these things out of his own strength rather than as an expression of the power of God. When this occurs, we act independently of the law of life and hence independently of the guiding thread that sustains human existence, and however good this independent action may appear to be from an external point of view, it is finally lawless because it fails to spring from a divine ground. The disguised wolf and the rotten tree thus become the prophet and the miracle worker who attempt to function independently of God and who reap the negative consequences of their own lawless and ungrounded behavior.

When the ungrounded natural consciousness says "Lord, Lord" on the last day, it will be rejected, for the last day of judgment is too late to establish a positive relationship with the ground of human existence. The phrase, "Lord, Lord," has only two possible functions, the first of which is to establish an initial link between time and eternity by accepting a divine gift. Thus, we can say with the tax-gatherer: "Lord, be merciful to me a sinner." The second positive function of this phrase, uttered against the background of the first, is simply to acknowledge that Jesus is Lord and that his lordship consists in the fact that he is the grounding source of power that sustains human life. The words in question cannot express a request to be acknowledged because of one's own good deeds, but can only be used to acknowledge the lordship of the one who has already made divine perfection fully accessible. As a result, the request for mercy and the acknowledgment of lordship are two sides of a single coin, the counterfeit versions of which are always condemned to ultimate destruction. Thus Jesus says to the disguised wolf and to the rotten tree that approach him with pride in their own good deeds, "Depart from me, you who practice lawlessness, for I never knew you."

CHAPTER XXI

TWO FINAL ANALOGIES: HOUSES, ROCK, AND SAND

🍎

In summarizing the content of the Sermon on the Mount, Jesus tells his followers that they must enter a narrow gate if they are to gain access to God's kingdom. He also speaks about a narrow pathway that can be identified with the Sermon itself and that leads us from the Beatitudes with which it begins to the sustaining source of power that undergirds the journey. Jesus warns his disciples that as they travel along this narrow path, a number of obstacles are to be encountered, the most dangerous of which is the disguised wolf. Wolves appearing in sheep's clothing will attempt to imitate the disciples behavior, but they will do so in order to lead them astray and finally to devour them. The disguised wolf is a counterfeit version of those who have chosen to enter the narrow gate, and the deceptive power they express is not the power of divine transformation, but an erotic power of their own that will attempt to consume the sheep they encounter. Two kinds of life are to be found along the narrow pathway, one of which is the radical inversion and the destructive corollary of the other.

In verses twenty-four through twenty-seven of the seventh chapter of Matthew, Jesus brings his Sermon to a conclusion by drawing a distinction between these two ways of living in terms of two analogies. In these verses he says:

> Therefore everyone who hears these words of Mine, and acts upon them, may be compared to a wise man, who built his house upon

the rock. And the rain descended, and the floods came, and the winds blew, and burst against that house; and yet it did not fall, for it had been founded upon the rock. And everyone who hears these words of Mine, and does not act upon them, will be like a foolish man, who built his house upon the sand. And the rain descended, and the floods came, and the winds blew, and burst against that house; and it fell, and great was its fall (Mt 7.24–27).

One of the most obvious things to notice about this passage is that the two kinds of listeners it describes have a great deal in common. In the first place, they both listen to what Jesus says, and they both hear the same message. In the second place, they are both engaged in the task of building, or as a contemporary thinker has expressed a similar point, they have both undertaken the task of building and dwelling.[1] The message of Jesus thus becomes the occasion for making a choice between two kinds of life and between two kinds of houses that we can build and occupy. The two houses under discussion in these verses point to two ways of living, for in both the Scriptures and in psycho-analytical theory, the houses we dream about and construct are to be identified with ourselves. As a result, these two listeners not only hear the same message, and are not only engaged in the same project of construction, but in each case, what is at stake is the kind of life they will build. Finally, engaged as they are in a common project, the two kinds of listeners to whom Jesus refers confront similar difficulties. Rain falls on them both; floods are encountered in both cases; and the winds of discord and tribulation blow against the kind of house that each is in the process of constructing.[2] Jesus concludes his Sermon with a realistic appraisal of the human condition, suggesting that we all stand on common ground with respect to hearing, building, dwelling, and confronting the discordant elements of human experience.

However much the two listeners Jesus mentions share common ground, it is nevertheless true that he draws a radical distinction between them. He says that one is wise and the other foolish, or in a more accurate formulation of the original text, that one displays practical wisdom and that the other is an idiot. The concept of wisdom mentioned here is not reducible to theoretical reflection, but points instead to prudent action demanded by concrete circumstances. In listening to the Sermon on the Mount, and in constructing a house appropriate to it, insight and theoretical understanding are clearly required. *Theoria* simply means to see things clearly, and as we have discovered already, Jesus clearly enjoins his followers to embrace vision of this kind. However, practical wisdom transcends theoretical reflection when what is at stake is building a life, and it is only when we are wise in this richer sense that the teaching of Jesus begins to make a practical difference in our experience and actions. By contrast, Jesus tells us that the one who listens without acquiring wisdom is a fool, and in making this claim, he uses the same word that he told us in Chapter Five never to use. In that context, Jesus says, "Whoever shall say, 'You fool,' shall be guilty enough to go into the hell of fire." However, in the passage before us, what is involved is a descriptive characterization of a bankrupt condition rather than an emotional outburst that issues in a personal indictment. As we move along the narrow pathway, our task is not to call another a fool, but to express the message of divine perfection that makes redemption possible. Nevertheless, the fact remains that the fool has said in his heart that there is no God and that his foolishness consists in his failure to make a positive response to the vertical dimension of human experience. The disciples do not have the right to cut another person off from this vertical dimension by calling him a fool, but if one hears the message of Jesus and fails to respond, *he is nevertheless a fool* because he has failed to embrace practical wisdom and to build his house upon a rock.

Jesus tells us that the wise man builds his house upon a rock, and as I have suggested already, the clear implication of this message is that the house in question is a human life. But what is the rock to which Jesus refers, and how is it related to the message he has just delivered? No doubt, the rock is Jesus himself, for as Stanley Jones reminds us, the intention of the Sermon on the Mount is to call our attention to the Christ on the Mount. However, there is also a respect in which the rock to which Jesus refers is the Sermon he has presented, for we find that his life is finally inseparable from the words he has spoken. Jesus suggests at the end of his message that if we have listened, if we have heard, and if we have responded positively, our lives are founded on a rock.

It is indeed paradoxical to describe the Sermon on the Mount as a rock, for on the surface, it does not appear to have the ring of solidity to it. "Blessed are the meek, for they shall inherit the earth"; "Blessed are those who are persecuted, for they shall be called the children of God"; "Love your enemies"; "Enter a narrow gate and walk along a narrow pathway"; and finally, "Be perfect as your Father in heaven is perfect." Are these words a rock upon which we can stand, or are they simply the expression of a slave mentality and of a utopian ideal? Does this message have a bearing upon the real order and provide a foundation for human existence within this context, or is it merely a picture of the infinite beyond, where the lion and the lamb will lie down together, detached from the weight and the solidity of human experience? (Is 11.6,7). In suggesting that the Sermon on the Mount is a rock, and in claiming that this rock is the foundation upon which human life can be built, Jesus rejects these other interpretations and calls us back to live within the real order. The paradox of the message is that it inverts the world, and that it implies that a life can be grounded only when this inversion has occurred. As a result, what appears to be a bifurcation between the real order and an ideal realm becomes the context where human life can be transformed and where it can be built upon an unshakable foundation.

The fact that Jesus is addressing his concluding remarks to followers who must live within the real order is suggested by his reference to the discordant elements they must confront. Rain comes down from above and batters human life; floods rise up from below and threaten to undermine our existence; and winds from all directions beat upon us, attempting to sweep our "houses" away. However, it is also instructive to notice that the only place left unmentioned is the center of our being, where the message of the Sermon on the Mount is intended to bring about a divine transformation. Jesus is assuring us that those who have listened and responded to his message can withstand anything because their lives have been inverted at the center and have been grounded on a rock. Again and again Jesus asks his followers to find the center of human existence and to turn away from the circumference around which we are so often inclined to spin. But now he reminds us that the center of life is the place where divine perfection can be encountered and that it is finally in terms of divine power that life itself can be built. The center of life is where God is to be found; the perfection of life is the maturity we can achieve when God's power is at work within; and the unshakable foundation upon which this maturing self-development can be grounded is the rock of Christ himself and the solidity that can be found in the words he speaks. Jesus tells us that the one who acts upon his teaching can be compared to a wise man who built his life upon a rock, so that when the rains descended, the floods came, and the winds beat upon it, it did not fall because it was grounded on the foundation of his life and message.

When Jesus tells us that the house of the wise man is founded upon a rock, the verb he uses is expressed in the passive voice. When we find the center of human existence and build our houses there, we do not ground ourselves, but are grounded instead by a divine reversal of the natural consciousness. If solid ground is to be found, the ravenous wolf within must be transformed into a poverty-stricken sheep, and it is on the basis of this divine transformation that mature self-development can begin. The natural consciousness is engaged in digging for a foundation that it can establish for itself, and when it strikes a rock, it often attempts to keep on digging in order to find a ground of its own making. However, Jesus suggests that when the rock reveals itself, our own digging must cease, and we must accept the fact that our lives can be founded upon a rock that displays a grounding power of its own. When God's divine power inverts the world, he invites us to invert the shovel with which we dig our way through the world, for it is only when we do so that we will have discovered a foundation that can sustain what we build. From that moment on, whatever we dig must be the expression of the power that we find in the rock, and the attempt to build a life upon it must be consonant with the fact that the foundation has already been laid by another. The passive voice of the verb in question points to the fact that the hardest work has already been accomplished, and the perfect tense of that same verb suggests that it has been accomplished once for all. As a result, building and dwelling presuppose a divine foundation, and the grounding act which allows us to find solid rock is an act that will sustain us clear to the end.

In the sixteenth chapter of Matthew, Jesus asks his disciples, "Who do people say that the Son of Man is?" (Mt 16.13–16). And they answered, "Some say John the Baptist; some, Elijah; and others, Jeremiah, or one of the prophets." But then Jesus said, "But who do you say that I am?" And Simon Peter replied, "Thou art the Christ, the Son of the living God." Finally, Jesus said in response:

> Blessed are you, Simon Barjona, because flesh and blood did not reveal this to you, but My Father who is in heaven. And I also say to you that you are Peter, and upon this rock I will build My church; and the gates of Hades shall not overpower it (Mt 16.17,18).

The name Jesus gives Simon Peter has two meanings. On the one hand, it means a rock, and on the other hand, a little pebble. In the moment in which Simon Peter recognized that his life was founded on the rock Christ provides, he himself became a rock and his faith became the foundation of a new kind of human community. Later on, when Peter attempted to deny his foundation, he became a pebble, and the foundation that he had embraced and come to imitate appeared to recede in the destruction and the scandal of the cross. However, when Simon met Jesus again by the Sea of Galilee and responded to the question, "Lovest thou me?" he became a rock again, and he rediscovered the foundation upon which his life could be built. By implication, he also rediscovered the truth of the Sermon on the Mount, where Jesus says that when the wise man builds his house upon a rock, the rains can descend, the floods can come, and the winds can beat upon it, but it can never be destroyed.

There is one dimension of Luke's account of this passage that Matthew fails to mention, but which ought to be taken into account. In verses forty-seven through forty-nine of Chapter Six Luke says:

> Everyone who comes to Me, and hears My words, and acts upon them, I will show you whom he is like; he is like a man building a house, who dug deep and laid a foundation upon a rock; and when a flood rose, the torrent burst against that house and could not shake it, because it had been well built. But the one who has heard, and has not acted accordingly, is like a man who built a house

upon the ground without foundation; and the torrent burst against
it and immediately it collapsed, and the ruin of that house was
great (Lk 6.47–49).

In this passage, we are not only given an account of the foundation of
the house, and of the negative elements it must confront, but are also
told that the house that is founded on a rock has been well-built.[3]
The task of growing toward maturity is not a task that can stop with
the discovery of a foundation, but must drive on until the house that
is erected upon it is complete. One of the problems with any commentary on the Sermon on the Mount is that it can tempt us to dwell
on the reflective level and lose ourselves in the powerful language to
be found in the Sermon itself. However, the crucial question to be
confronted about the message is not primarily reflective or rhetorical, but the much more fundamental question about what kind of
house we will build upon the foundation it provides. When Jesus
calls our attention to a rock, he points beyond reflection and language to life itself, and in Luke's formulation, he suggests that the life
to which he leads us must be well-built as an expression of divine
perfection in the real order.

In our earlier discussion, we have found that there is always a
realistic dimension in what Jesus says, and we find that dimension
once more in his account of the two kinds of houses. Jesus does not
simply conclude by referring to the wise man who builds his house
upon a rock, but points to the much more frequent phenomenon of
the foolish man who builds his life upon the sand. The natural consciousness is always inclined to keep on digging, but when it digs in
the sand it is caught up in an infinite project that will never come to a
satisfactory conclusion. In fact, one might be inclined to build his life
upon the sand, not because he prefers sand to solidity, but because he
has committed himself *to the infinite project of digging*. Digging one's
way through the world can be a degenerate expression of building
and dwelling. However, Jesus says that if we choose to live in this
way, we are fools, for the infinite project that seeks to become God
by its own action can never withstand the rain, the floods, and the
winds that are bound to come. The infinite quest for a foundation of
one's own will always meet an infinite resistance, and the result will

be that the house or the life built according to a pattern of this kind will always be destroyed. Thus Jesus tells us in verses twenty-six and twenty-seven:

> And everyone who hears these words of Mine, and does not act upon them, will be like a foolish man, who built his house upon the sand. And the rain descended, and the floods came, and the winds blew, and burst against that house; and it fell, and great was its fall (Mt 7.26,27).

Indeed, the crash is great and is also tragic beyond measure, for Jesus came to make it possible for us to build our houses on a rock. Moreover, he came to make it possible for us to avoid the destruction that always comes when we seek to build our lives upon the unstable foundation of our own infinite activity.

In Matthew's version of the Sermon on the Mount, there are two more verses that allow the writer to place brackets around the message that has finally come to a conclusion. At the beginning of the Sermon, Matthew brackets his account by referring to the multitudes that had been following Jesus, and by allowing Jesus to move away from them, generates a space that Jesus intended his disciples to cross. The Sermon itself begins on this basis, and it moves us away from the Beatitudes of Chapter Five to the concluding story about the kinds of houses at the end of Chapter Seven. When this conclusion has been reached, the multitudes appear again, moving gradually across the space that had separated them from Jesus and his followers. They have their own response to make to what they have overheard at a distance, and Matthew brings his account of the Sermon on the Mount to a conclusion by recording their reactions. In verses twenty-eight and twenty-nine of Chapter Seven, Matthew says:

> The result was that when Jesus had finished these words, the multitudes were amazed at His teaching; for He was teaching them as one having authority, and not as their scribes (Mt 7.28,29).

Matthew says that the multitudes were amazed at Jesus' teaching, or in a literal translation of the same word, he tells us that they were "awestruck" by what they had heard. This should not be surprising, for the Sermon as a whole was intended to provoke amazement then, just as it does today. Jesus came to Galilee proclaiming the kingdom of God, but he did so in an unexpected fashion, suggesting that poverty of spirit was necessary to gain entrance to it. The crowds had expected to be freed from their shackles and from their oppression, but they were introduced instead into a kingdom where meekness, purity of heart, and persecution are the central themes. Jesus also shocked his audience by suggesting that the Law not only needed to be obeyed, but also needed to be fulfilled. This claim, which echoes and re-echoes through Chapter Five, is shocking because it suggests that the Law can be perfected, and indeed, that it will be transcended by the content of Jesus' own teaching. As Jesus formulates the point, the Law does not stand upon its own foundation, but is an expression of the grace of God. Jesus says, "You have heard that it was said . . . , but I say unto you," pointing by implication to the divine transformation that the grace of God can produce at the center of our being. Jesus then points to the center of human existence where a transformation is required in the most shocking sentence to be found in the entire Sermon. In verse forty-eight of Chapter Five he says, "Be perfect, just as your Father in heaven is perfect."

The kingdom Jesus proclaimed is not what the audience had expected; the Law that they had been obeying did not provide its own fulfillment but needed to be fulfilled; and now Jesus says that this same audience must be perfected by embracing the kind of maturity that God the Father has already displayed. In Chapter Six and in the first six verses of Chapter Seven, Jesus points to six specific regions where divine perfection can be expressed, pointing by implication to the ways in which our own actions in these regions can easily degenerate. In the process, he shocks his audience by reinterpreting the meaning of giving, praying, and fasting; by reformulating what it means to lay up treasure, what it means to see, and what it means to follow God as master; and by pointing to the need to transcend anxiety and to outstrip the judgmental tendencies that often alienate us from one another. Finally, Jesus shocks his audience by claiming that if they are to become citizens of God's kingdom, they must enter by a narrow gate, and must walk along a narrow pathway. Moreover, he tells them that they must be prepared to penetrate the disguise of the wolf dressed in sheep's clothing, and that having done so, they must build their lives upon God's foundation rather than upon a foundation of their own making.

Though Matthew tells us that the multitudes were amazed at Jesus' teaching, he does not suggest that many of them believed. However, if belief is to be possible, it will be grounded upon another characteristic of Jesus teaching which the multitudes also recognized. As Matthew says in verse twenty-nine, they were amazed at his teaching because "he was teaching them as one having authority, and not as their scribes." What is the authority that Jesus displayed, and upon the basis of which belief in him would be a reasonable response? In the first place, "authority" means "power and lordship," and indeed, it is authority in this sense that is reflected most clearly throughout the course of the message. However, the striking fact about the word "authority" is that it also means "freedom." Jesus taught with authority, not simply because he displayed power and lordship, but also because he brought liberation to the human soul.[4] If the Law places us in bondage, the grace of God expressed in the message of Jesus sets us free. And if the anxiety that besets us threatens to destroy us, the divine perfection to which he gives us access allows us to participate in the freedom of God's perfect peace. Finally, the word "authority" points to the originative moment in which one enters God's kingdom and to the sustaining source of power that this originative moment makes accessible. The Author is the Originator, and it is on the basis of this fact that freedom can be received and lordship and power can be acknowledged. Jesus taught as one having power; he taught as one who brings freedom; but most fundamentally, he taught as the one who stands at the origin of human existence and as the one who can bring transformation to the human soul.

NOTES

Chapter 1

[1] *The Illustrated Bible Dictionary,* vol. 3 (Wheaton, Illinois: Tyndale House Publishers, 1980), 1417–19.

[2] Referring to Matthew as "The First Book of the New Revelation" and noting that the Sermon on the Mount takes place on a mountain, Norman Perrin says: "Matthew is stressing the parallel to Moses receiving the Torah on a mountain, the previous revelation now being superseded (Exod. 19:3–6)" (*The New Testament: An Introduction* [New York: Harcourt Brace Jovanovich, Inc., 1974], p. 179).

[3] Clarence Jordan, *Sermon on the Mount* (Valley Forge, Pa.: Judson Press, 1980), pp. 9–11.

[4] E. Stanley Jones, *The Christ on the Mount* (New York: The Abingdon Press, 1931), p. 11.

[5] Plato, *Republic,* vol. 2, trans. Paul Shorey (Cambridge: Harvard University Press, The Loeb Classical Library, 1969), 2.368e–2.369a.

[6] Jones, pp. 27–28.

[7] *Ibid.,* p. 38.

[8] *Ibid.,* pp. 41–42.

Chapter 2

[1] Aristotle, *Nicomachean Ethics,* in *The Complete Works of Aristotle: The Revised Oxford Translation,* vol. 2, ed. Jonathan Barnes (Princeton, New Jersey: Bollingen Series LXXI·2, Princeton University Press, 1984), 1095a16–1102a4 and 1176a30–1181b24.

²Jordan, pp. 19–20.

³Aristotle, *Nicomachean Ethics*, 1098a16 and 1178a5–9.

⁴Jones, pp. 52–53.

⁵Jordan, p. 20.

⁶*Ibid.*, p. 21.

⁷Augustine, *Confessions*, in *Augustine: Confessions and Enchiridion*, trans. Albert C. Outler (Philadelphia: Westminster Press, 1955), p. 251, f.n. 24.

⁸Nietzsche says: "The saint in whom God delights is the ideal eunuch. Life has come to an end where the 'kingdom of God' begins" (*Twilight of the Idols*, in *The Portable Nietzsche*, ed. and trans. Walter Kaufmann [New York: Penguin Books, 1982], p. 490).

⁹Jones, pp. 67–69.

Chapter 3

¹*Ibid.*, p. 72.

²Anders Nygren, *Agape and Eros*, trans. Philip S. Watson (Philadelphia: The Westminster Press, 1953), pp. 105–109.

³Jones, p. 72.

⁴*Ibid.*, p. 73; and Jordan, p. 22.

⁵In *The Antichrist*, Nietzsche asserts:

A critique of the *Christian conception of God* forces us to the same conclusion. . . . Now he becomes a sneak, timid and modest; he counsels "peace of soul," hate-no-more, forbearance, even "love" of friend and enemy. He moralizes constantly, he crawls into the cave of every private virtue, he becomes god for everyman, he becomes a private person, a cosmopolitan (*The Portable Nietzsche*, pp. 582–583).

⁶Jones, p. 74.

Chapter 4

¹Jones, p. 76.

²Dag Hammarskjöld, *Markings*, trans. Leif Sjöberg and W. H. Auden (New York: Ballantine Books, 1983), p. 83.

Chapter 5

¹Jones, p. 86.
²*Ibid.*, pp. 87–89; and Jordan, pp. 40–42.
³Jones, p. 91.
⁴*Ibid.*, p. 97.

PART II

Chapter 6

¹"God intends to save a race," Jones states. And therefore, "before the final revelation in Christ we find ideas being implanted in the human mind wherever it would open in order that men could undertand them when they came in their perfection and completion"—the righteousness of the Hebrew, illumination of the Greek, loyalty of the Japanese, and so on. The most-loved characteristic of a people can be recognized in Christ and affirmed in a Christian life. "And yet it is not a composite. The plant reaches down into the soil and takes out elements akin to its own nature. But the end is not a patchwork of heterogeneous elements. It is a new living thing, for the laws of the life of the plant determine the disposition of the elements taken from the soil. Thus the gospel reaches down into the soil of each nation and picks out elements akin to its own nature. . . . The gospel repudiates syncretism, it refuses eclecticism, but it does assimilate, for it is life" (pp. 101–110).

Chapter 7

¹*Ibid.*, pp. 131–134.
²In a discussion of *Psalm* 53:1 with his friend Evodius, Augustine also points beyond foolishness by first referring to the Septuagint Version of *Isaiah* 7:9b: "Unless you believe, you shall not understand." [Translated more pertinently in the New American Standard Version this passage reads: "If you will not believe, you surely shall not last."] He then declares: "Our Lord Himself, by His words and deeds, first urged those whom He called to salvation to believe. . . . Then to those who believed, he said, 'Seek and ye shall find.' [*Matthew* 7:7] For what is believed without being known cannot

be said to have been found, and no one can become fit for finding God unless he believes first what he shall know afterwards" (*On Free Choice of the Will*, trans. Anna S. Benjamin and L. H. Hackstaff [Indianapolis, Indiana: Bobbs-Merrill Educational Publishing, 1980], pp. 38–39.)

[3]Jordan, footnote, p. 50.

Chapter 8

[1]Jones, pp. 148–149.

[2]*Ibid.*, p. 153.

[3]T. W. Manson, *The Teaching of Jesus* (Cambridge: University Press, 1963), pp. 292–295.

Chapter 9

[1]Augustine, *Soliloquies,* in *Augustine's Early Writing,* Ichthus Edition, trans. John H. Burleigh (Philadelphia: The Westminster Press, 1st ed. 1953), pp. 59–60.

[2]Jones, p. 159.

Chapter 10

[1]Jordan, pp. 63–65.

[2]Jones, pp. 172–173.

[3]*Ibid.*, p. 177.

[4]*Ibid.*, p. 173.

[5]As Jones say, "Jesus himself did not give the man his request when he asked him to divide his brother's inheritance, but he did give to him—he gave him something that he needed more than the inheritance, namely, sound teaching about covetousness [Luke 12:13–59]" (p. 167).

Chapter 11

[1]See especially 30:31–33 of Augustine's *On Christian Doctrine,* trans. D. W. Robertson, Jr. (Indianapolis and New York: The Bobbs-Merrill Com-

pany, Inc., 1958), pp. 25–27; and his Sermon 2, 6–8 in *On Psalm 31*, as cited by
Vernon J. Bourke, *The Essential Augustine* (Indianapolis: Hackett Publishing
Company, 1983), pp. 187–189.

  [2]Nygren emphasizes this point several times. See *Agape and Eros*,
pp. 125–126, pp. 132–133, and pp. 139–140.

  [3] In *Beyond Good and Evil*, even Nietzsche says, "What is done out of
love always occurs beyond good and evil" (*The Portable Nietzsche*, p. 444).
And in *Ethics*, Dietrich Bonhoeffer claims that for the Pharisee "every moment of life becomes a situation of conflict in which he has to choose between
good and evil," and that these men "cannot confront any man in any other
way than by examining him with regard to his decisions in the conflicts of
life." By contrast, Bonhoeffer states:

> No one can discern in Jesus the uncertainty and the timidity of one
> who acts arbitrarily, but His freedom gives to Him and to His
> followers in all their actions a peculiar quality of sureness, unques-
> tionableness and radiance, the quality of what is overcome and of
> what overcomes. The freedom of Jesus is not the arbitrary choice of
> one amongst innumerable possibilities; it consists on the contrary
> precisely in the complete simplicity of His action, which is never
> confronted by a plurality of possibilities, conflicts or alternatives,
> but always by one thing. This one thing Jesus calls the will of God.
> He says that to do this will is His meat. This will of God is His life.
> He lives and acts not by the knowledge of good and evil but by the
> will of God. There is only one will of God. In it the origin is
> recovered; in it there is established the freedom and the simplicity of
> all action. . . . God's revelation in Jesus Christ, God's revelation of
> His love, precedes all our love towards Him. Love has its origin not
> in us but in God. Love is not an attitude of men but an attitude of
> God (ed. Eberhard Bethge [New York: Macmillan Publishing Co.,
> Inc., 1978] pp. 27, 30, and 51).

PART III

Chapter 12

  [1]Jones, pp. 199–201.
  [2]Ernest M. Ligon, *The Psychology of Christian Personality* (New
York: The Macmillan Company, 1936), pp. 165–166.

³Jordan, p. 76.
⁴Jones, p. 210.

Chapter 13

¹Carl G. Vaught, "Two Meditations on Love," *The Drew Gateway,* vol. 53, no. 1 (Fall, 1982), 31.
²Soren Kierkegaard, *Fear and Trembling* and *The Sickness Unto Death* (Garden City, New York: Doubleday, 1954), pp. 46, 51, 57.
³Augustine, *Confessions,* p. 51.
⁴Carl G. Vaught, *The Quest for Wholeness* (Albany, New York: State University of New York Press, 1982), pp. 72–92.
⁵Edward Schillebeeckx, *Jesus: An Experiment in Christology,* trans. Hubert Hoskins (New York: The Seabury Press, 1979), pp. 652–669.
⁶According to J. N. Geldenhuys and F. F. Bruce:

The petition 'Thy kingdom come' may, for general purposes, be used as a supplication that the divine dominion (*basileia*) of God will be extended 'here and now' (in this present age) in the heart of individuals as well as in the world as a whole. Primarily, however, this petition has an eschatological connotation; it is a supplication that the kingly rule of God may be established 'with power' (Mk. 9:1) at the glorious appearing of the Son of man. . . . The third petition, 'Thy will be done on earth as it is in heaven,' . . , has a partial reference to the present age, but it opens up vistas to the time when every knee shall bow before the King of kings and the powers of darkness will be finally destroyed. God will then be all in all and his will shall reign supreme (1 Cor. 15:25–28). The three imperatives *hagiasthētō* ('be hallowed'), *elthatō* ('come') and *genēthētō* ('be done') are all aorist and point to the final consummation (*The Illustrated Bible Dictionary,* vol. 2, pp. 910–911).

⁷Citing A. Wilkenhauser, R. V. G. Tasker states:

It would seem reasonable to suppose that the 'first' Gospel was not given the primary place in the New Testament solely because it was believed to embody some of the earliest gospel material to be committed to writing. It was also, to judge from the frequency with which it was quoted by Christian writers in the second century, their favourite Gospel. Indeed, as Wilkenhauser has pointed out, 'in the time of Irenaeus the Church and Christian literature were more deeply influenced by the Gospel of Matthew than by any other New Testament book' (p. 158). It became known as the 'ecclesiastical' Gospel, because it provided the Church with an indispensable tool in its threefold task of defending its beliefs against attacks from Jewish opponents, of instructing converts from paganism in the ethical implication of their newly-accepted religion, and of helping its own members to live a disciplined life of fellowship based on the record of the deeds and words of their Lord and Master, which they heard read week by week in the orderly and systematic form provided by this evangelist. In short, the Gospel of Matthew served as an apology, a handbook of instruction, and a lectionary for use in Christian worship (*New Testament Introduction* [1958], in *The Tyndale New Testament Commentaries: The Gospel According to St. Matthew,* gen. ed. R. V. G. Tasker [Grand Rapids, Michigan: Wm. G. Eerdmans Publishing Company, February, 1975], pp. 17–18).

Chapter 14

[1]As I express this point in *The Quest for Wholeness*:

The religion of the Hebrews brings the concepts of uniqueness and particularity to focus more clearly than does any other tradition in our history. . . . The world of Abraham, Isaac, and Jacob is individual, not universal, and it receives its concrete expression in the historical existence of a particular religious community. However, it is important to focus on this tradition because it emphasizes the particularity that is always involved in man's relationship with what is ultimate and because reflection upon it will make it possible for us to acknowledge the particularity to be experienced in our own case. . . . Through an imaginative identification with Abraham and his descendents, we can cross the space that separates us from the concept of origins, and in the process, can stand face to face with ourselves and with the originative ground of our existence. The Biblical story points beyond itself to a real ground, and it exhibits a dimension of depth that must always be acknowledged in silence. Yet we shall also find that appropriate reflection upon it will allow us to break beyond the bounds of universality and will permit us to make an intelligible response to what is unique about our own existence (pp. 49–50).

²Jordan, pp. 78–79.

³Jordan suggests that "fasting" means to "move fast" toward a dominating objective—a quest for knowledge, wanting to serve God, gaining money, and so on. And if taking time to shave, prepare food, even sleep, slows one down, he will forego those things in pursuit of his goal. But such abstinances may be perverted to win praise and admiration and so become an end in themselves. Jordan also points to the paradigm of "fasting" to be found in John 4:31–34, where Jesus is so caught up in telling the Samaritan woman at the well about the source of perfection that his disciples have to tell him to eat the food for which he himself had sent them (p. 79).

Chapter 15

¹G. B. Caird, in reference to Mt. 6:21 ("our hearts being where our treasure is"), notes that since the ancients knew nothing of the function of the brain, they "spoke of the heart as the seat of thought" (*The Language and Imagery of the Bible* [Philadelphia: The Westminster Press, 1980], pp. 66–68). Caird's interpretation makes all the more compelling Bonhoeffer's account in *The Cost of Discipleship*:

> Wordly possessions tend to turn the hearts of the disciples away from Jesus. What are we really devoted to? That is the question. Are our hearts set on earthly goods? Do we try to combine devotion to them with loyalty to Christ? Or are we devoted exclusively to him? The light of the body is the eye, and the light of the Christian is the heart. If the eye be dark, how great is the darkness of the body! But the heart is dark when it clings to earthly goods, for then, however urgently Jesus may call us, his call fails to find access to our hearts. Our hearts are closed, for they have already been given to another. As the light cannot penetrate the body when the eye is evil, so the word of Jesus cannot penetrate the disciple's heart so long as it is closed against it. The word is choked like the seed which was sown among thorns, choked "with cares and riches and pleasures of this life" (Luke 8:14). The singleness of the eye and heart corresponds to that "hiddenness" which knows nothing but the call and word of Christ, and which consists in perfect fellowship with him (trans. R. H. Fuller [New York: Macmillan Publishing Co., Inc., 1979], p. 193).

²Jones, p. 227; Jordan, p. 92.

3Jones, p. 231; Jordan, p. 93; and Bonhoeffer, *Discipleship*: "If our hearts are entirely given to God, it is clear that we *cannot* serve two masters" (p. 195).

4Jones, pp. 228–229.

Chapter 16

1Augustine, *Confessions,* pp. 172–173.

2Jones, pp. 232–231.

3Jordan, pp. 95–96.

4 Jones, pp. 233–234.

5In this passage, this point is illustrated with reference to Moses in the following way:

Because his vision of the past and the future is so clear, Moses' . . . inability to go into the Promised Land is not a loss of wholeness. In fact, his acceptance of his finitude is a crucial element in the wholeness he achieves. The limitation imposed upon him points to the fact that his place within the Hebrew community must be taken by another and that wholeness within the Hebrew tradition can only be achieved by a developing community of participants. This endless task is an image of the mystery and the openness of the concept of wholeness and a reflection of the mystery and the openness of God himself. The individuality of Moses also requires that he accept his limits, for it is only by accepting the fact that he cannot enter the new land that Moses lives and dies with his own space intact. Moses' existence within the larger community is defined in the face of limitations—limitations that allow him to bind the past and the future of his own life together in a finite unity. However, at this final moment, it must not be forgotten that Moses is not only a finite individual, but that he also stands before God and that he is buried with God's own hands. At the end of his life, Moses returns to his origins at both the horizontal and vertical levels, and it is in this respect that his quest for wholeness is finally brought to fulfillment (Vaught, *The Quest for Wholeness,* pp. 91–92).

Chapter 17

1Jordan, pp. 102–103.

²Jones, pp. 246–247.
³*Ibid.*, pp. 249–250.

PART IV

Chapter 18

¹Jones, p. 266.
²*Ibid.*, pp. 278–281; Jordan, p. 112.
³Jones, p. 257; Jordan, pp. 113–114.

Chapter 19

¹According to Jones, what is termed "the Golden Rule" should be called "the Golden Principle" since Jesus never gave rules of life.

Rules are soon outgrown, for they are made to fit local situations, which rapidly change. Since principles are the same yesterday, today, and forever, they are never outgrown. We make rules out of principles, to fit changing situations. The rules change but the principles do not. In a religion founded on rules, . . . one of two things happens: either the people in growing break the rules or the rules break the people. Jesus therefore wisely gave no rules of life, but he did give principles, which are capable of living amid changing and advancing civilization and are never outgrown. This Golden Principle is one of them. We are to treat others as we would like to be treated were we in their place. That principle will never be outgrown either in heaven or on earth (p. 284).

²Jordan, pp. 115–116.
³Aristotle, *Nicomachean Ethics* (1106b28–33. Or as Montaigne would later reformulate the point: "If falsehood, like truth, had only one face, we would be in better shape. For we would take as certain the opposite of what the liar said. But the reverse of truth has a thousand shapes and a limitless field" (*Essays,* 1.9, in *The Complete Works of Montaigne,* trans. Donald M. Frame [Stanford, California: Stanford University Press, 1967], p. 24).

Chapter 20

¹According to Charles Sanders Peirce:

> Every sane person lives in a double world, the outer and the inner world, the world of percepts and the world of fancies. . . . A man can be durably affected by his percepts and by his fancies. The way in which they affect him will be apt to depend upon his personal inborn disposition and upon his habits. Habits differ from dispositions in having been acquired as consequences of the principle, virtually well-known even to those whose powers of reflection are insufficient to its formulation, that multiple reiterated behaviour of the same kind, under similar combinations of percepts and fancies, produces a tendency—the *habit*—actually to behave in a similar way under similar circumstances in the future. Moreover—*here is the point*— . . . *reiterations in the inner world—fancied reiterations—if well-intensified by direct effort, produce habits,* just as do reiterations in the outer world; *and these habits will have power to influence actual behaviour in the outer world* (*Philosophical Writings of Peirce,* ed. Justus Buchler [New York: Dover Publications, Inc., 1955], pp. 283–284).

"The parish of percepts," Peirce adds, "is not inside our skulls, either, but out in the open. It is the external world that we directly observe" (*Ibid.,* 308).

Chapter 21

¹Martin Heidegger, *Poetry, Language, Thought,* trans. Albert Hofstadter (New York: Harper & Row, Publishers, 1975), pp. 145–161.
²Jones, pp. 315–317; Jordan, pp. 122–123.
³Jones, p. 316; Jordan, pp. 122–123.
⁴Jones, p. 316; Jordan, pp. 123–124.

INDEX

Adultery: Pharisees' interest in the problem of, 77–78; woman taken in, 78–79

Agape: and friendship, 110; as necessary condition for philia, 71–72

Anger: its meaning in the Greek text, 66

Anointing the head: symbol of God's presence, 136

Anxiety: and the grace of God, 148–149; fruitless attempts to guarantee the future, 154; implicates both soul and body, 148; indeterminacy and pervasiveness, 147; Jesus' awareness of our external needs, 151–153; most difficult of human questions, 147; reason for Jesus' concern with the problem, 147–148; results from two incompatible ways of living, 147; sources, 147; spatial and temporal dimensions, 150–151; story of the Fall, 151

Aristotle: concept of happiness, 13–14; the unity of truth, 210

Augustine: definition of the self, 125; his discussion of the fool, 67–68; faith seeking understanding, 203–204; God and the soul in the thought of, 91; interpretation of the Good Samaritan story, 109

Beatitudes: as blessings, 13; blessings and cursings, 13; developmental dimension of the first three, 21–22; and happiness, 13; as ethical prescriptions, 38; as expressions of the grace of God, 38; as expressions of a relationship with God, 39; the fourth a dynamic version of the first, 26; given in the midst of persecution, 40; their inner and outer dimensions, 40; logical structure of the first six, 29–30; in the Old Testament, 13; their outward thrust, 23; two ways to read them, 38

Being seen versus being noticed: as a central problem, 118–119; oscillation between sin and good deeds, 119–120; rewards from God, 120

Body: and flesh, 83

Central purpose of human action: God's glory, 118–119

Condemnation: separation from God, 79

Daily bread: translation of the phrase, 130–131

Debt: transgressions, 133–134; two meanings, 131–132

Disciples of Jesus: their character, 6; relation to their master, 7

Discordant elements to be confronted: rain, wind, and floods, 193–194

Divine inheritance: John's description of it in Revelation, 22

Divorce: contrast between Matthew and Mark about, 86–88; and forgiveness, 89; Jesus' teaching not a universal law, 88; marriage triangle and the problem of, 87; and mixed marriages, 89; Old Testament context for the problem of, 84–85; Paul's conception of, 88–89